Arabic Script

Part 2 of
Let's Talk Arabic

الكتابة العربية

Dr. Adam Yacoub

http://www.LetsTalkArabic.com

This title is also available at major online book retailers.
© Copyright 2011 Adam Yacoub
ISBN-13:978-1467981460
ISBN-10: 146798146X
All rights reserved. No part of this publication may be reproduced, stored in a retrieval system, or transmitted, in any form or by any means, electronic, mechanical, photocopying, recording, or otherwise, without the written prior permission of the author.

DEDICATION

I wish to thank all of those who have kindly helped with introducing this book, every effort or advice have been made to trace all the covered topics but if any had been inadvertently overlooked the author will be pleased to make the necessary arrangement at first opportunity

Contents

Acknowledgments	
Preface	3
Unit one: The Letters	7
The Letters Short Vowels	10
THE SHORT VOWEL-MARKS	14
The long vowels	15
Write over the letters	16
sukun and shaddah	45
Arabic letters – Joined Form	46
Reading Exercises	52
Silent letters in Arabic	55
UNIT TWO	58
What's This?	59
Useful Adjectives	62
Grammar notice	65
Saying (to have) in Arabic	71
Arabic - English glossary	76
English - Arabic glossary	88

ACKNOWLEDGMENTS

We are lucky enough to have benefited from the experience of some of the experts in teaching Arabic across this edition. We would like to thank everyone for his or her useful comments on this work.

Part 2

Preface
Congratulations

mabrook

Well done for making such a decision to learn the Arabic language. For whatever reason it may be, a new challenge, relocation to an Arabic speaking country or for business, you can rest assured that you have made another great decision in choosing one of the most successful and smoothest Arabic courses. This book will lead you to push yourself and take a step above the rest in a fun and interactive way.

Arabic is considered to be one of the most alive, important and beautiful languages in the world. This book uses an extremely stimulating, logical and easy way to help you learn from the very beginning. In any language, speaking appears to be the most fundamental aspect for a lot of people. From the start of the book, you will be introduced to the basics of speaking and pronunciation, using a simple format that allows everyone to speak Arabic in a natural way. The book will then continue to develop your new skills by enabling you to understand and heighten your ability to read, listen to and write this amazing language.

Arabic is a Semitic language and is the formal and official language of 22 Arab countries. It is also the spoken language of almost 420 million people living in Arabic and non Arabic countries.

This book will teach you the basics of Modern Standard Arabic (MSA), which is the modernization of the Classical Arabic structures, as well as additions from the main dialects spoken all over the Arab world.

Variations of the Language

Like any other language, spoken Arabic has some dialects with variations and differences. The differences between these dialects are incomprehensible from one to the other, and can be referred to as five main dialects divided according to their regions.

Maghreb

The Maghreb dialect is spoken in the region of the Maghreb countries, Libya, Tunisia, Algeria, Mauritania, and Morocco.

Egyptian:

The Egyptian dialect is used in Egypt, Sudan, Yemen, and some western parts of Saudi Arabia. It is the most widely understood colloquial dialect across the Arab world, because almost 93% of Arabic Movies, TV, and Media use the Egyptian dialect.

Levantine

The Levantine dialect comes from and is used in Lebanon, Palestine, Jordan and Syria.

The Gulf

The Gulf dialect is spoken in the Arabic Gulf Countries, which are made up by Iraq, Kuwait, most of Saudi Arabia, Qatar, Bahrain, the United Arab Emirates, and Oman.

Modern Standard Arabic

MSA (Modern Standard Arabic) has become the most popular dialect and is now spoken and used by all the Arab countries.

The dark countries on the map show the Arab League.

Written Arabic

The core of Arabic writing that is used today comes from the classical Arabic which is principally defined as the Arabic used in the Qur'an and in the earliest form of literature from the Arabian Peninsula.

Two Important Facts

The First is that, any language has a vast wealth of vocabulary, but do we need to learn that vast amount to be able to communicate in a language?

Of course not! **Just, 20%** of the words in a language make up to **80%** of the conversations we face in our daily life. You may not be speaking like a native immediately, but you'll have a solid base and the ability to keep improving and developing yourself. This method is suitable for everyone from frequent travelers to first timers, as well as language students and enthusiasts.

So, this book focuses on the vital 20% that will help you speak Arabic interactively and dynamically.

The second point and this is a really exciting fact. The Arabic language uses word roots, for example, we can take one root like (**KTB**) from the word (**KaTaBa**) which means "he wrote" and from there conjugate all **Arabic verbs tense.** Nouns can also be made from the same root because they have a relation with it.

KaaTeB= writer,   **KeTaab**= book,   ma**KTaB**= office,

ma**KTaBa**= library,   ma **KToob** = letter & written,   and more.

Arabic grammar is fairly simple compared to Western languages, but the language itself has richness in its vocabulary that exceeds most languages in the Western world.

UNIT 1

THE LETTERS

Arabic writing is an alphabetic script, based upon distinct characters, adjoined to other characters, which almost look like ***the English cursive way of writing***, but Arabic is written from right to left, not left to right.

The Arabic alphabet has **28** letters, 3 of which have vowel qualities, but it's not fair to say that they are 28 letters. In fact they are only 15 shapes and dots, these dots play an essential role in distinguishing the difference between the shapes.

The following Arabic letters do not have any correspondence in the Latin alphabet. For example: kh (equals German ch), gh (a softer version of kh).

ʿayn (guttural stop, but clearly pronounced from the back of the throat), th (as in English).

dh (softer version of th), sh (as in English) and strong and emphasized versions of the letters **t, d, s, z, h.**

One letter, called hamza, is not even pronounced, other than as a glottal stop. In transcriptions it is marked with a ' only.

Below is the Arabic alphabet and key to show you how to pronounce them. Try to read paying attention to the pronunciation.

The letter	Pronunciation
ا Alif ('a)	As in (a); apple, absolutely, April, and like (a): man, hat, mat.
ب Ba' (b)	As in (b); bat, band, balcony.
ت Ta' (t)	As in (t); tank, tab.
ث Tha' (th)	Like (th); thank, three, throat, thin, think, thief.
ج Jeem (j)	As in (j): Jam, jack, jacket.
ح (H) Not in English	A rough, aspirated ' H ' (as when you swallowed something hot), or when you breath after running or doing sports
خ Kha' (kh)	As in (loch) in Scottish English accent,
د Dal (d)	As in (d); dad, door, dean.
ذ Thal (Th)	Like (th): they, father, mother, brother, together, feather.
ر Ra' (r)	As in (r): run, role, real.
ز Zai (z)	As in (z): zoo, zone.
س Seen (s)	As in (s): sat, sink, soon.
ش Sheen (sh)	Like (sh): shark, she, shy, Sharon.
ص Saad (S)	Heavy consonant of (s) like: son, summer.
ض Daad (D)	Heavy consonant of (d) like in: done, duck
ط Taa' (T)	Heavy consonant of (T) like: Tariq, tall, tower

ط (TH) Not in English	Heavy consonant of the letter (z), sounds similar to although
ع (A) Ain	Not in English, it's roughly like (ai) in main but stronger
غ (gh) ghain	Like the French (**r**)
ف (f) Fa'	As in (f): farm, film, fogy, family
ق (q) qaf	Like (q): Qatar, Qur'an, quality.
ك (k) Kaf	Like (k): kind, king, Kuwait.
ل (l) lam	As in (l): lamp, lane, language.
م (m) Meem	As in (m): man, milk, moon.
ن (n) Noon	As in (n): now, new, nominal.
ه (h) Ha'	Like (h): hand, hair, here, honey, hear.
و (w) waw	Like (o): one, and (o) in: moon, more.
ي (y) Yaa'	Like (y): you, yesterday, and like (i) in: him, drink, Friday.

The Letters Short Vowels

Arabic is written from right to left, each Arabic letter has three ways of being pronounced and this is determined by the vowel that is above or below that letter.

For example: The letter - **alif**

- If there is a slash above (ا َ); this slash known as **Fat-Ha**.

- If the slash is below (ا ِ); this is known as **Kasra**.

- If a mark which looks like an apostrophe is used (ا ُ); we call this **Damma**, meaning it is pronounced with that short vowel mark.

The following table shows how to pronounce each letter with these marks.

ا َ *Aa*	ا ِ *e*	ا ُ *u*
as in أَب *Abb* = father	as in اِبْن *ebn* = son	as in أُمّ *Umm* = mother
بَ *Ba*	بِ *Be*	بُ *Bu*
بَنْك *bank* = Bank	As in بِنت *bent* = girl	as in بُرْج *burj* = tower
تَ *ta*	تِ *te*	تُ *tu*
as in تَمام *tamaam* = perfect	as in تِلك *telk* = that (feminine)	as in تُونس *tuunis* = Tunisia
ثَ *tha*	ثِ *the*	ثُ *thu*
as in ثَلج *thalj* = ice	as in ثِمَار *themaar* = flowers	as in ثُرَيّا *thurayya* = a star
جَ *Ja*	جِ *Je*	جُ *Ju*
as in جَزيرة *jazeera* = Island	as in جِنّ *jenn* = jinn	as in جُمْعَة *jum'a* = Friday

حَ Ha	حِ He	حُ Hu
as in حَسَن Hassan = good	As in جِنّة Hen-na = henna	as in حُسين Husain = Husain
خَ Kha	خِ Khe	خُ Khu
as in خَليج Khaleej = gulf	as in خِلال khelal = during	as in خُروج khuruj = Exit
دَ da	دِ de	دُ du
as in دَرْس dars = lesson	as in دِرهَم derham = Dirham	as in دُبي dubai = Dubai
ذَ Tha	ذِ The	ذُ Thu
as in ذَهَب Thahab = gold	as in ذِنْب The'b = wolf	as in ذُرَة thura = corn
رَ Ra	رِ Re	رُ Ru
as in رَأس ra's = head	as in رِيال reyal = riyal	as in رُكْن rukn = corner
زَ Za	زِ Ze	زُ Zu
as in زَهْرَة Zahra = rose	as in زِحام zehaam = crowd	as in زُهور zuhour = roses
سَ sa	سِ se	سُ su
as in سَلام salaam = peace	as in سِنّ senn = tooth	as in سُوق souq = market
شَ Sha	شِ She	شُ Shu
as in شَرْق sharq = east	as in شِتاء sheta' = winter	as in شُغْل shughl = work

صَ Sa	صِ Se	صُ Su
as in صَحْن SaHn = dish	as in صِحّة SeHHa = health	as in صُبْح SubH = morning
ضَ Da	ضِ De	ضُ Du
as in ضَبّ Dabb = lizard	as in ضِرْس Ders = molar	as in ضُمّ Dumm = join
طَ Ta	طِ Te	طُ Tu
as in طَريق Tareeq = road	as in طِفْل Tefl = child	as in طُرُق Toroq = roads
ظَ THa	ظِ THe	ظُ THu
as in ظَنّ THann = doubt	as in ظِفْر THefr = nail	as in ظُهْر THuhr = noon
عَ Aa	عِ ae	عُ O
as in عَمّان Amman	as in عِراق Iraq	as in عُمان Oman
غَ Gha	غِ Ghe	غُ Ghu
as in غَانا Ghana	as in غِنْوة ghenwa = song	as in غُروب ghurub = sunset
فَ Fa	فِ Fe	فُ Fu
as in فَمّ famm = mouth	as in فِيلم Felm = film	as in فُول fuul = beans
قَ Qa	قِ Qe	قُ Qu
as in قَطَر Qatar	as in قِطّ qett = cat	as in قُرْءان Qur'an
كَ Ka	كِ Ke	كُ Ku
as in كَلْب kalb = dog	as in كِتاب ketaab = book	as in كُويت Kuwait

لَ La	لِ Le	لُ Lu
as in لَبَن *laban* = milk	as in لِسان *lesaan* = tongue	as in لُغَة *lugha* = language
مَ Ma	مِ Me	مُ Mo
as in مَلِك *malik* = king	as in مِياه *meyah* = water	as in مُحَمّد *muhammad*
نَ Na	نِ Ne	نُ Nu
as in نَاس *naas* = people	as in نِصْف *nesf* = half	as in نُور *nuur* = light
هَـ Ha	هِـ He	هُـ Hu
as in هَات *haat* = bring	as in هِيَ *heya* = she	as in هُوَ *huwa* = he
وَ Wa	وِ We	وُ Wu
as in وَلَد *walad* = boy	as in وحدة *weHda* = unit	as in وُرود *wuruud* = flowers
يَ Ya	يِ Ye	يُ Yu
as in يَد *yad* = hand	as in يِن *yen* = yen	as in يُسْر *yusr* = easiness

THE SHORT VOWEL-MARKS

The three vowel-marks also have **doubled forms**. This creates a difference in pronunciation from the normal vowel-marks to an added '-n' sound . as below:

1- Whilst the (Fat-ha) makes the 'a' sound the (Fat-hatain) = (doubled form) makes the 'an' sound., for example

خً	حً	جً	ثً	تً	بً	اً
khan	Han	jan	than	tan	ban	an

continued this way for the rest of the letters.

2- Whilst the (kasra) makes the 'e' sound the (kasratain) = (doubled form) makes the 'en' sound., for example:

| Khen | Hen | jen | then | ten | ben | en |

continued this way for the rest of the letters.

3- The (damma) then makes the sound (u) and the (dammatain) makes the (un) sound, it's represented by a Damma with a slight inward 'tail' and is written above the letter as below:

خٌ	حٌ	جٌ	ثٌ	تٌ	بٌ	أٌ
Khun	Hun	jun	thun	tun	bun	un

The long vowels

The long vowels are a combination of doubled of short vowel marks, they are also seen as letters used to lengthen the sound of the vowel, for example;

1- Alif al-madd (ا) is the long vowel of the sound of the Fat-ha from 'a' into 'aa'. As in:

خا	حا	جا	ثا	تا	با	أ
Khaa	Haa	jaa	thaa	taa	baa	aa

Write over the letters below, the continue copying.

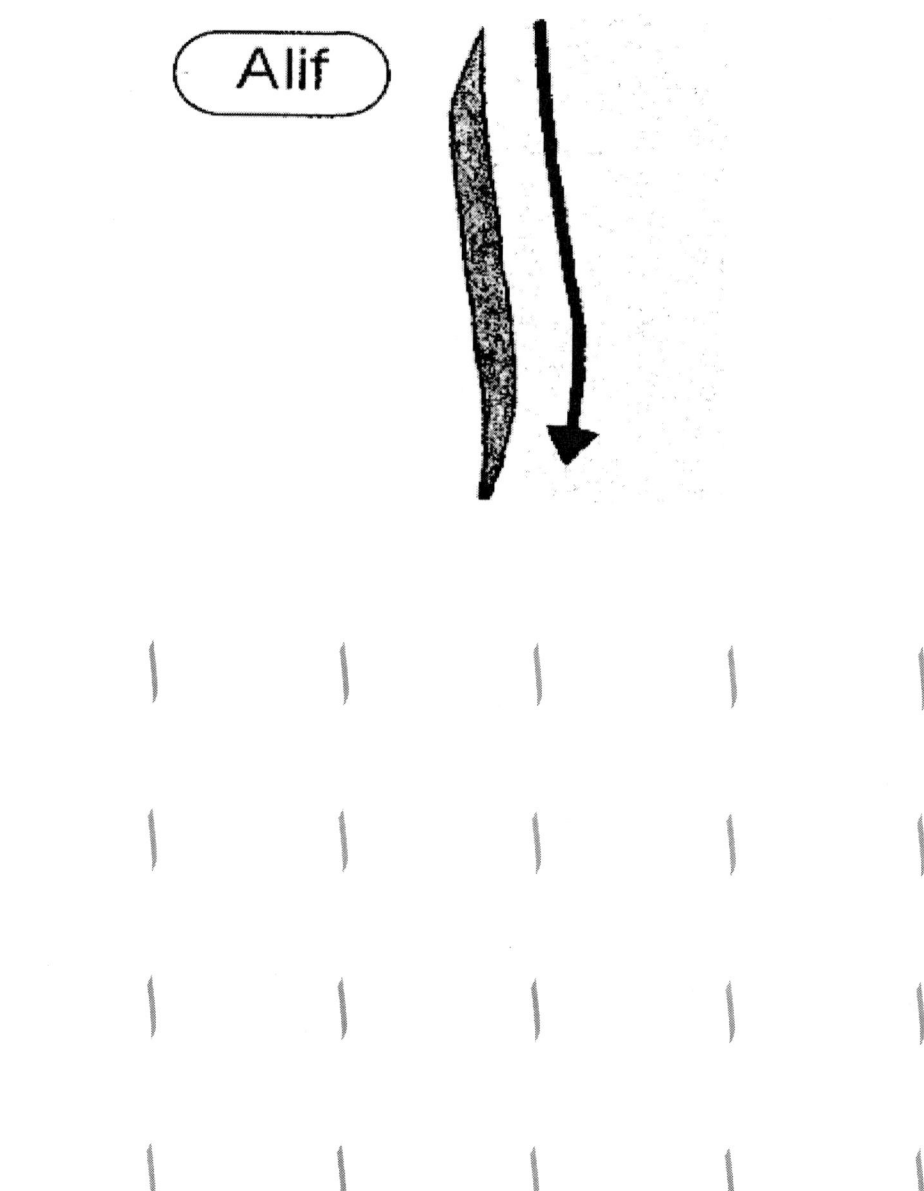

ا   ا   ا   ا   ا   ا

ا   ا   ا   ا   ا   ا

ا   ا   ا   ا   ا   ا

ا   ا   ا   ا   ا   ا

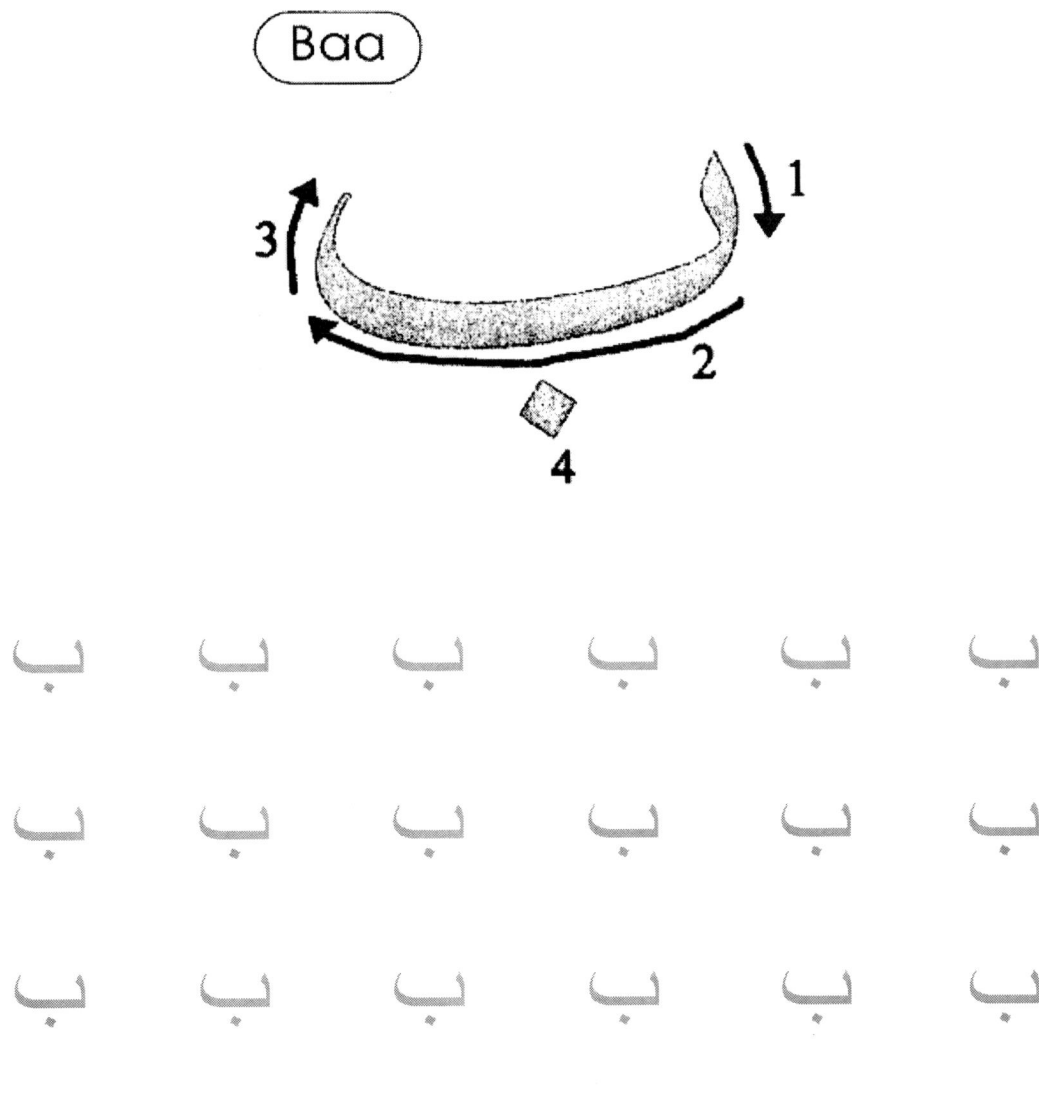

ب ب ب ب ب ب

ب ب ب ب ب ب

ب ب ب ب ب ب

ب ب ب ب ب ب

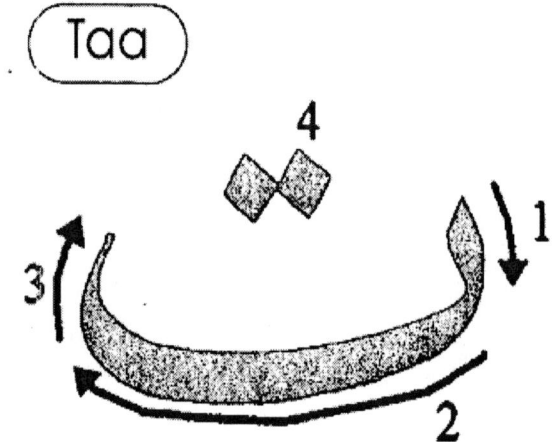

ت ت ت ت ت ت

ت ت ت ت ت ت

ت ت ت ت ت ت

ت ت ت ت ت ت

Arabic Script

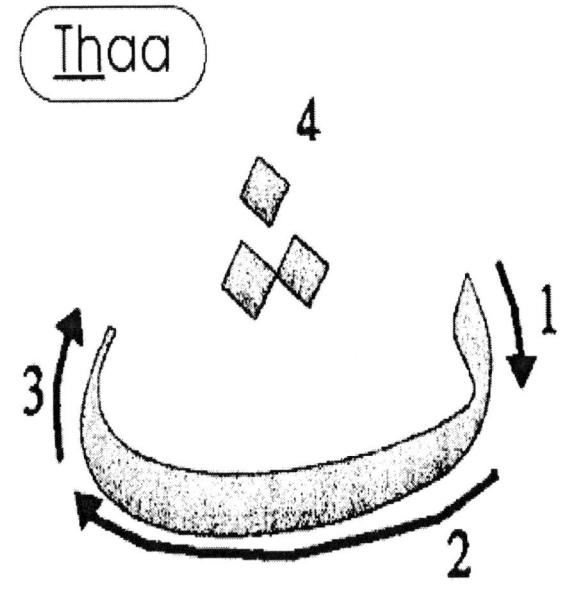

Thaa

ث ث ث ث ث ث

ث ث ث ث ث ث

ث ث ث ث ث ث

ث ث ث ث ث ث

ج ج ج ج ج ج

ج ج ج ج ج ج

ج ج ج ج ج ج

ج ج ج ج ج ج

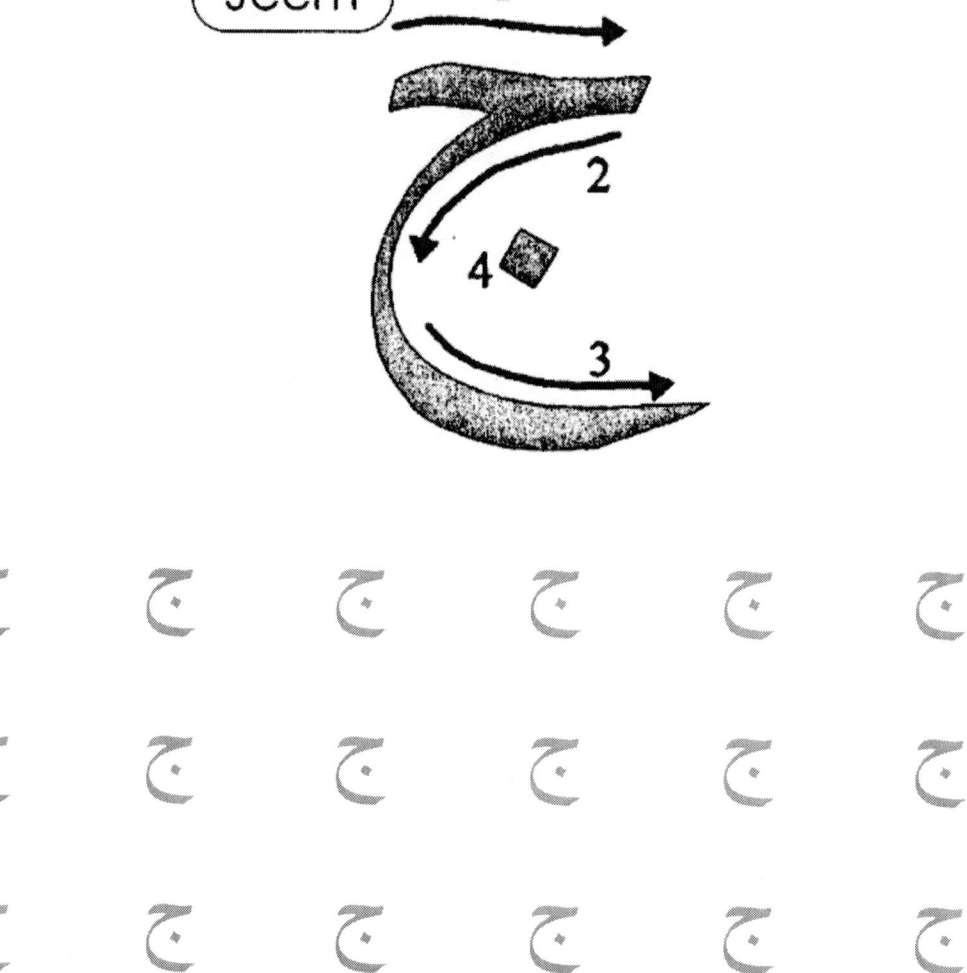

Arabic Script

ﺥ ﺥ ﺥ ﺥ ﺥ ﺥ

ﺥ ﺥ ﺥ ﺥ ﺥ ﺥ

ﺥ ﺥ ﺥ ﺥ ﺥ ﺥ

ﺥ ﺥ ﺥ ﺥ ﺥ ﺥ

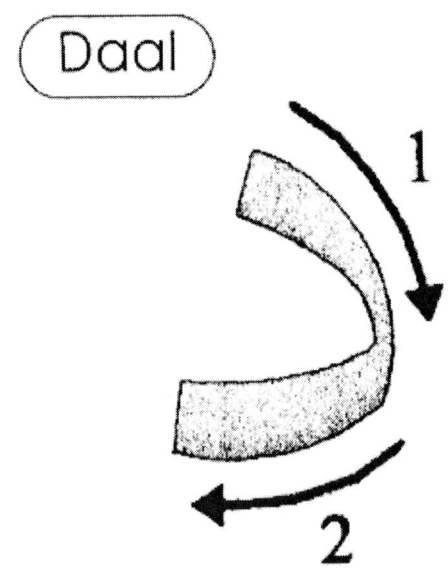

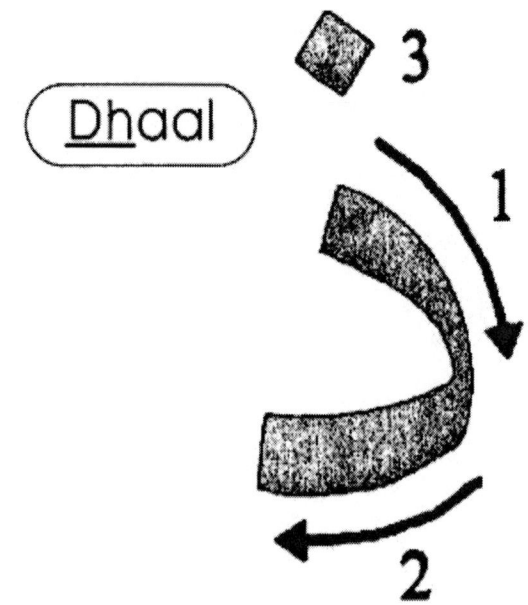

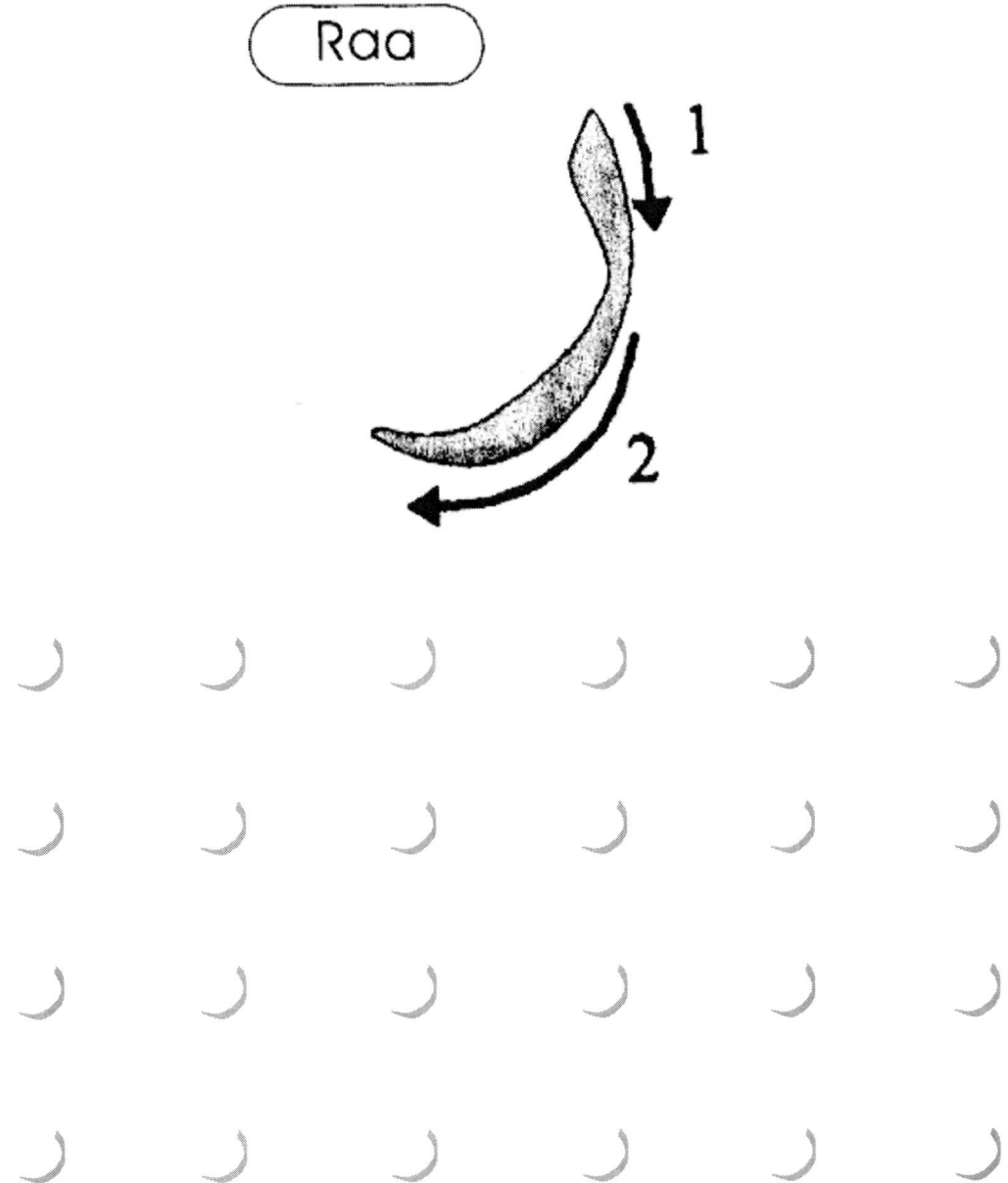

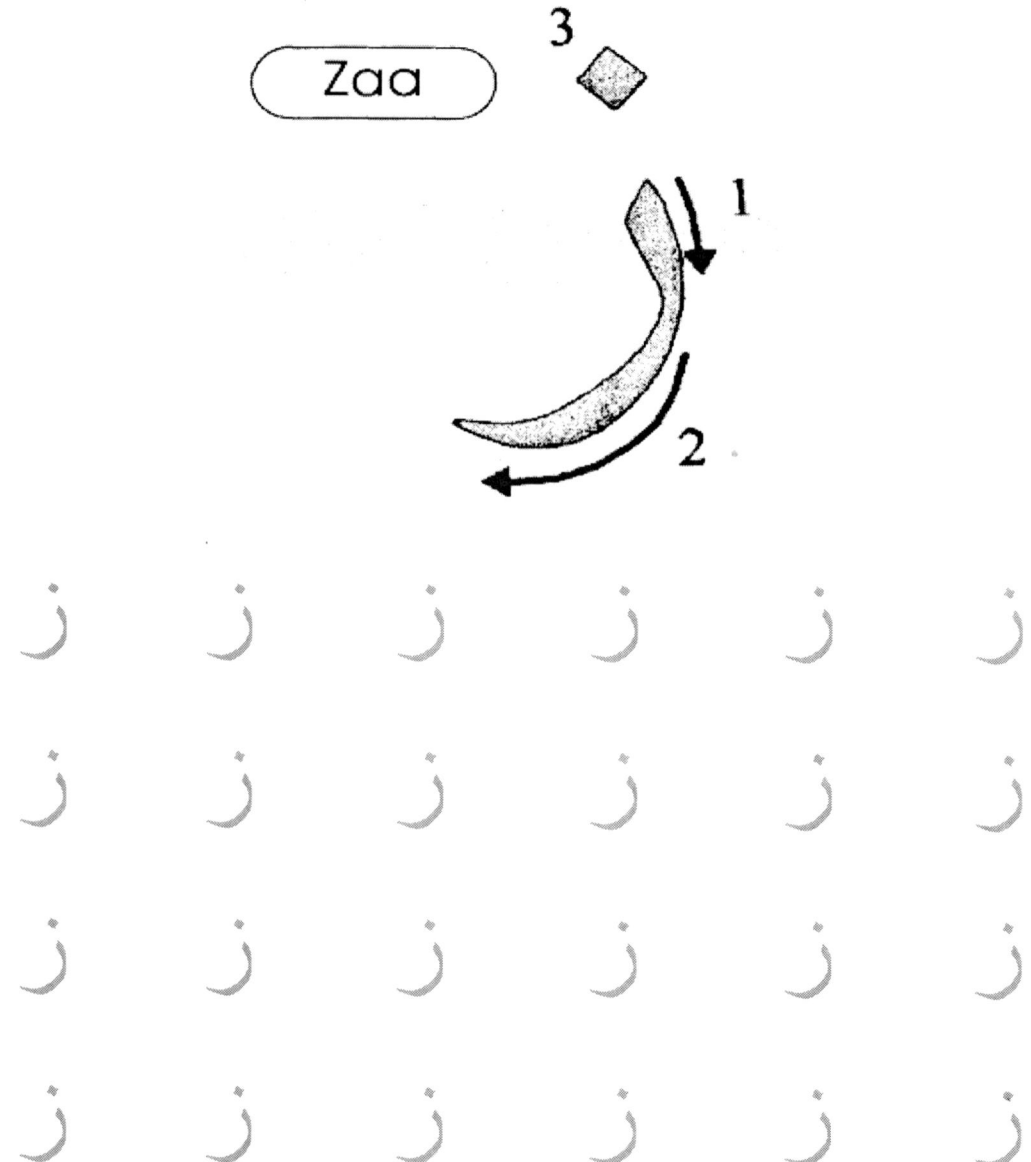

Seen

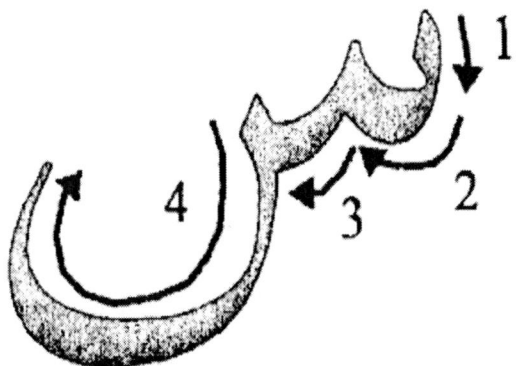

س س س س س س

س س س س س س

س س س س س س

س س س س س س

Arabic Script

Sheen

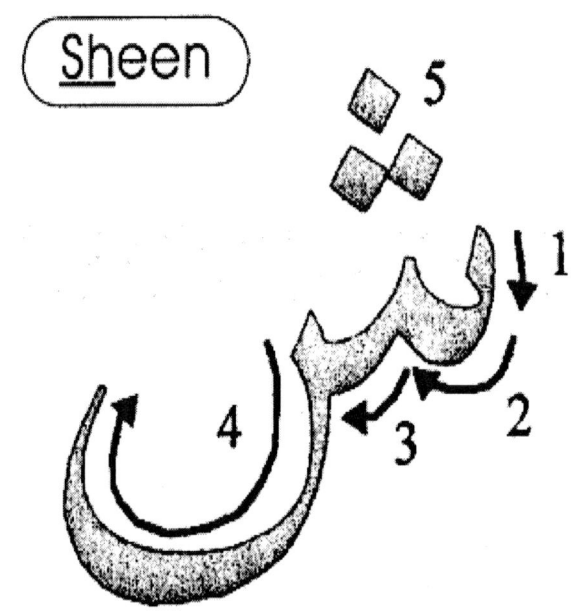

ش	ش	ش	ش	ش	ش
ش	ش	ش	ش	ش	ش
ش	ش	ش	ش	ش	ش
ش	ش	ش	ش	ش	ش

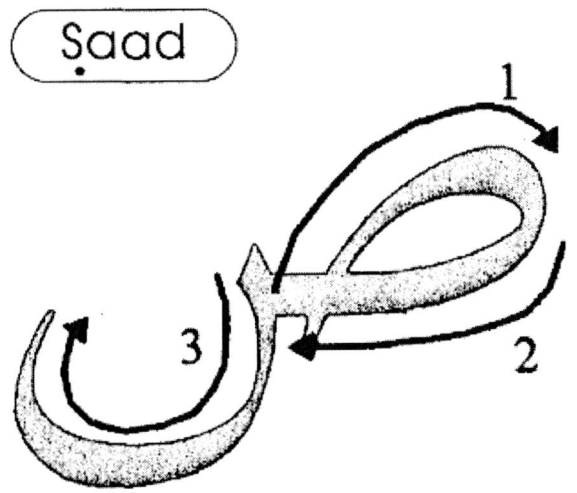

ص ص ص ص ص ص

ص ص ص ص ص ص

ص ص ص ص ص ص

ص ص ص ص ص ص

Daad

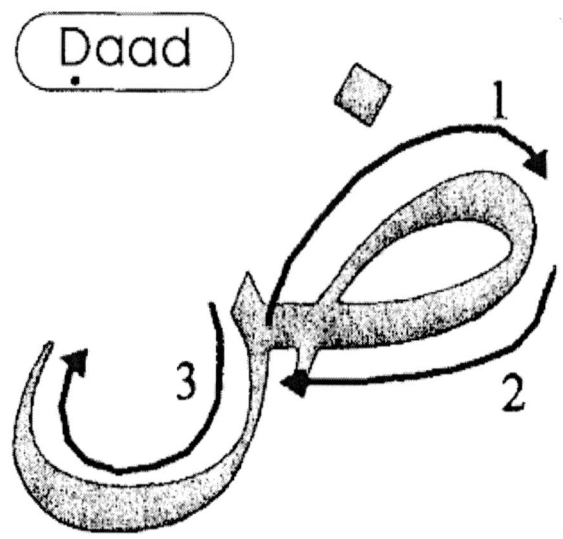

ض ض ض ض ض ض ض

ض ض ض ض ض ض ض

ض ض ض ض ض ض ض

ض ض ض ض ض ض ض

Ṭa

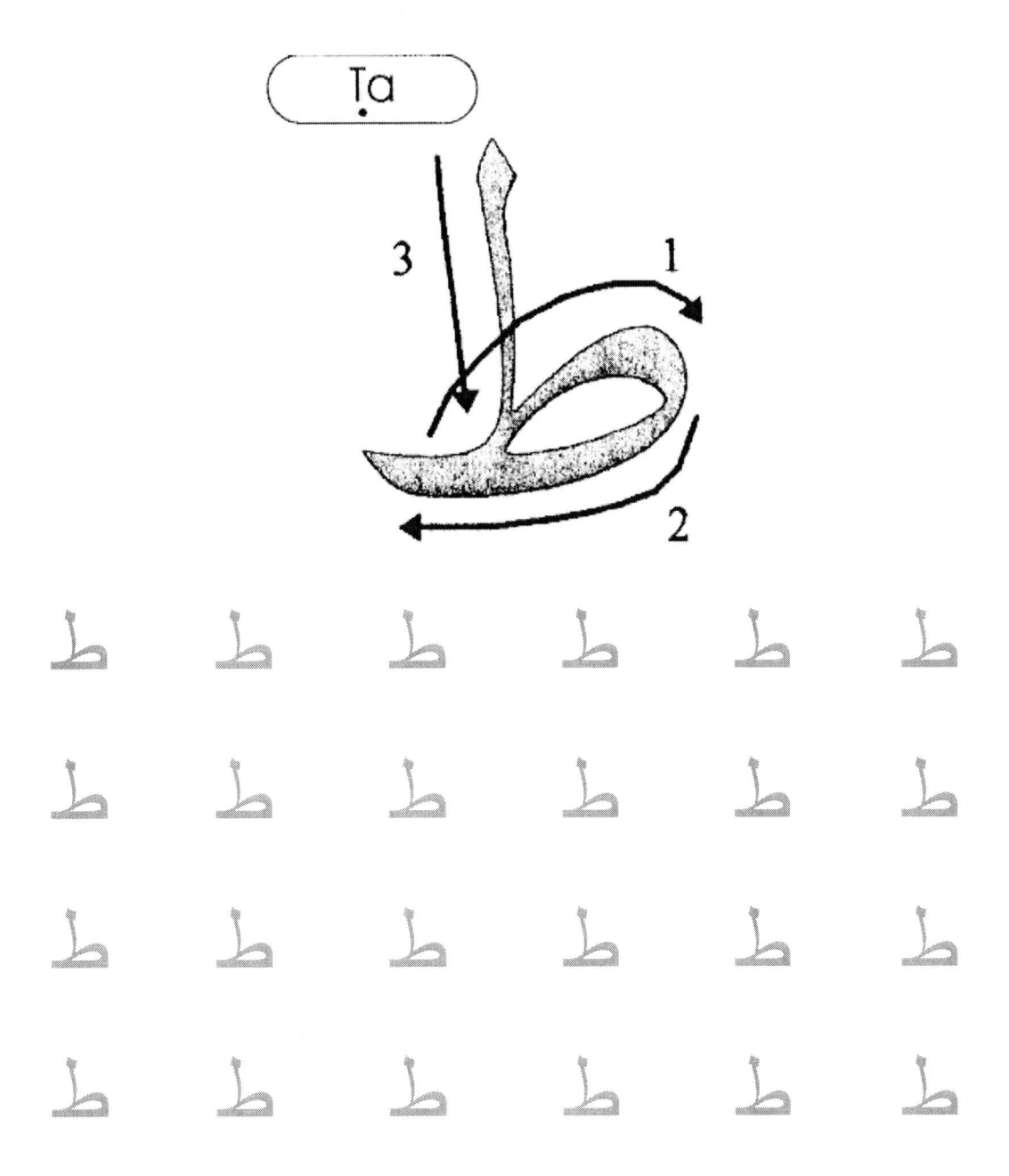

Arabic Script

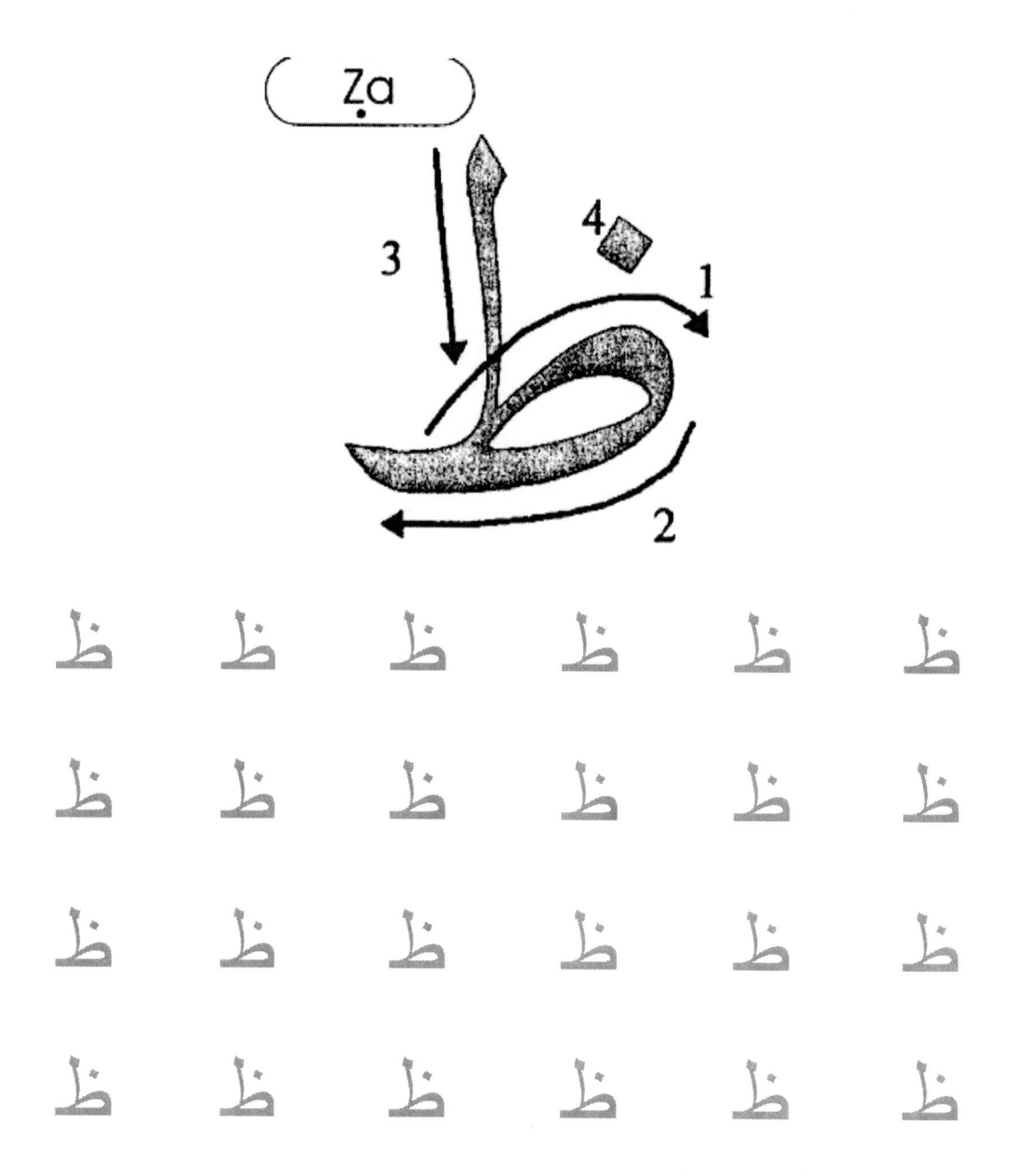

Ẓa

Arabic Script

ʿAyn

ع ع ع ع ع ع

ع ع ع ع ع ع

ع ع ع ع ع ع

ع ع ع ع ع ع

Ghayn

غ غ غ غ غ غ

غ غ غ غ غ غ

غ غ غ غ غ غ

غ غ غ غ غ غ

Faa

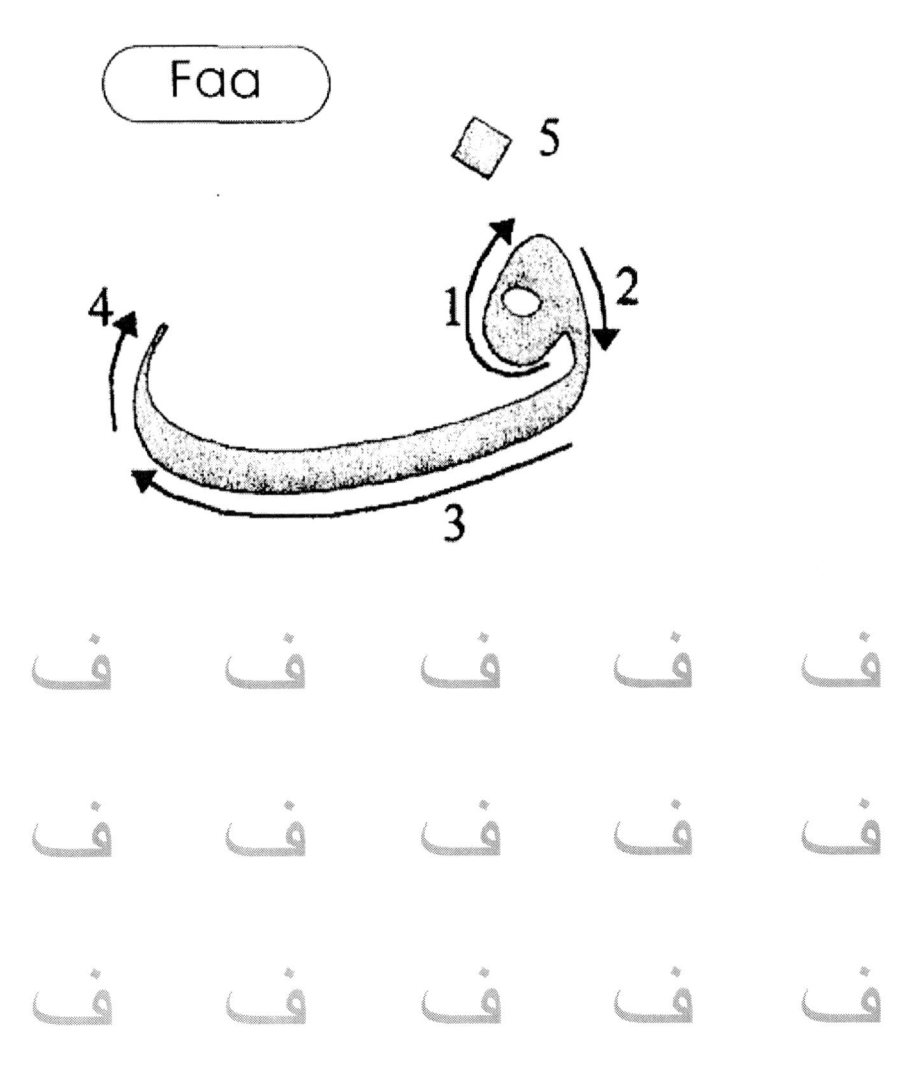

ف ف ف ف ف ف ف

ف ف ف ف ف ف ف

ف ف ف ف ف ف ف

ف ف ف ف ف ف ف

Qaaf

ق ق ق ق ق ق

ق ق ق ق ق ق

ق ق ق ق ق ق

ق ق ق ق ق ق

Arabic Script

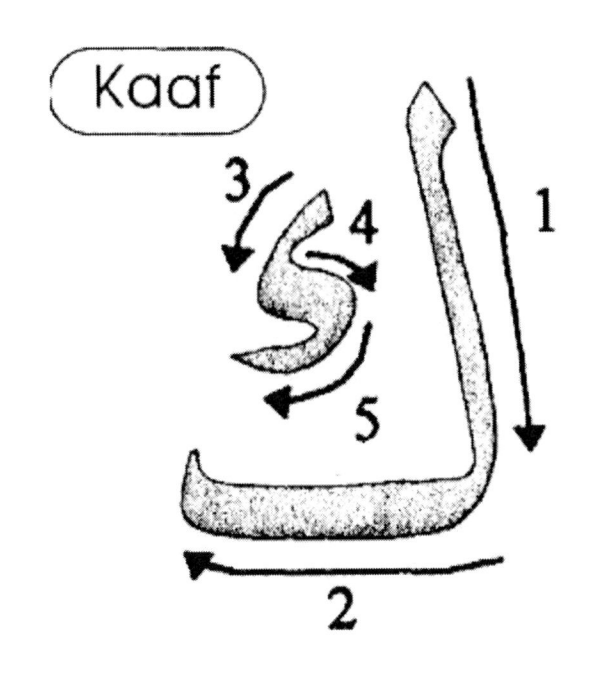

Kaaf

ك ك ك ك ك ك

ك ك ك ك ك ك

ك ك ك ك ك ك

ك ك ك ك ك ك

Laam

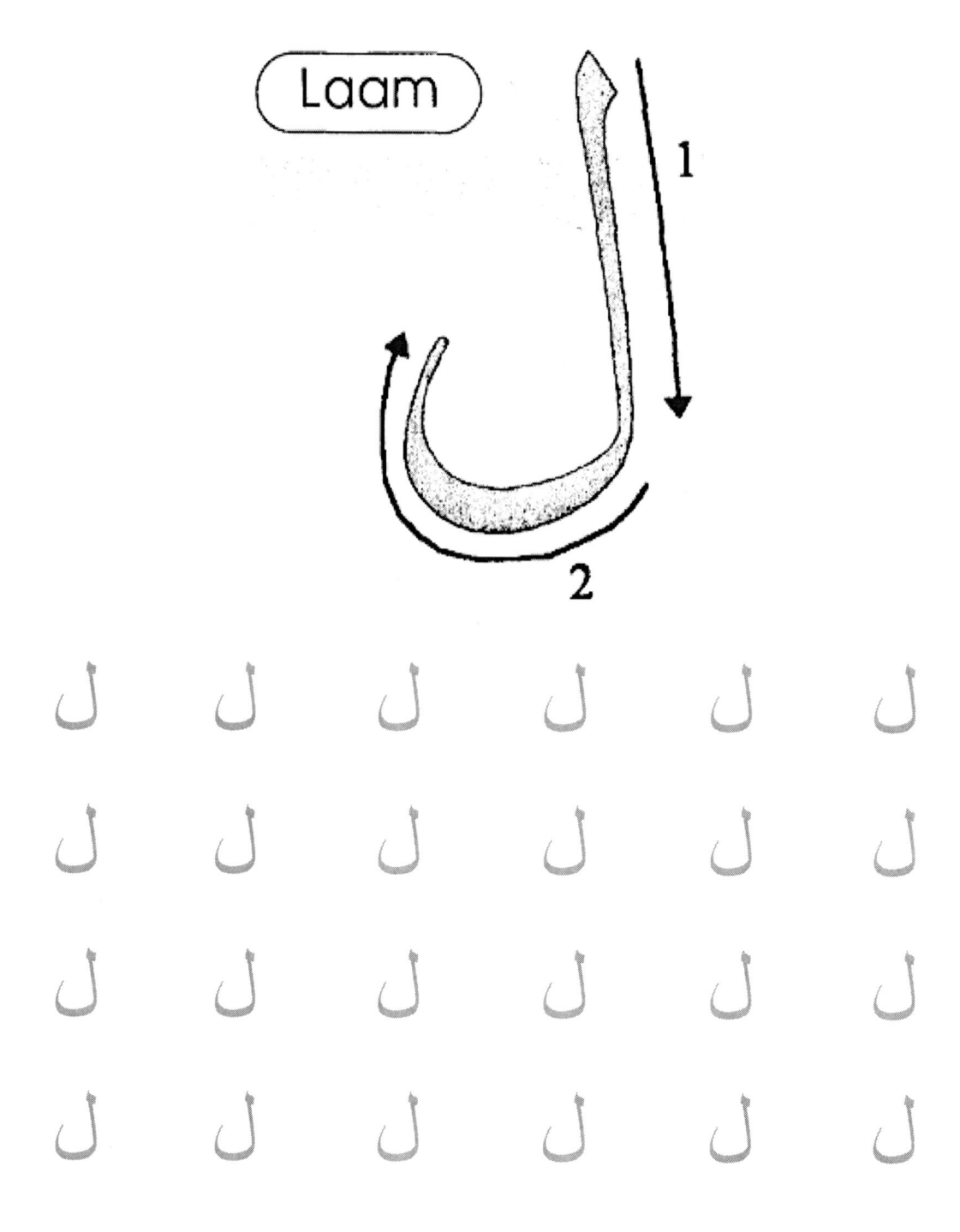

Meem

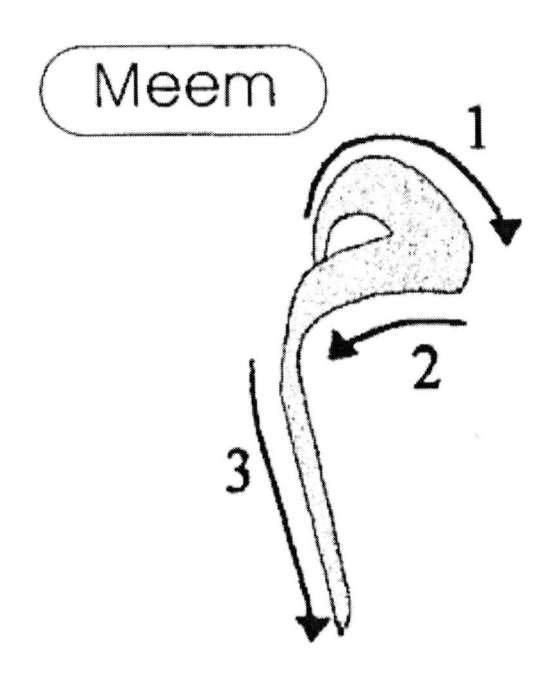

م م م م م م

م م م م م م

م م م م م م

م م م م م م

Arabic Script

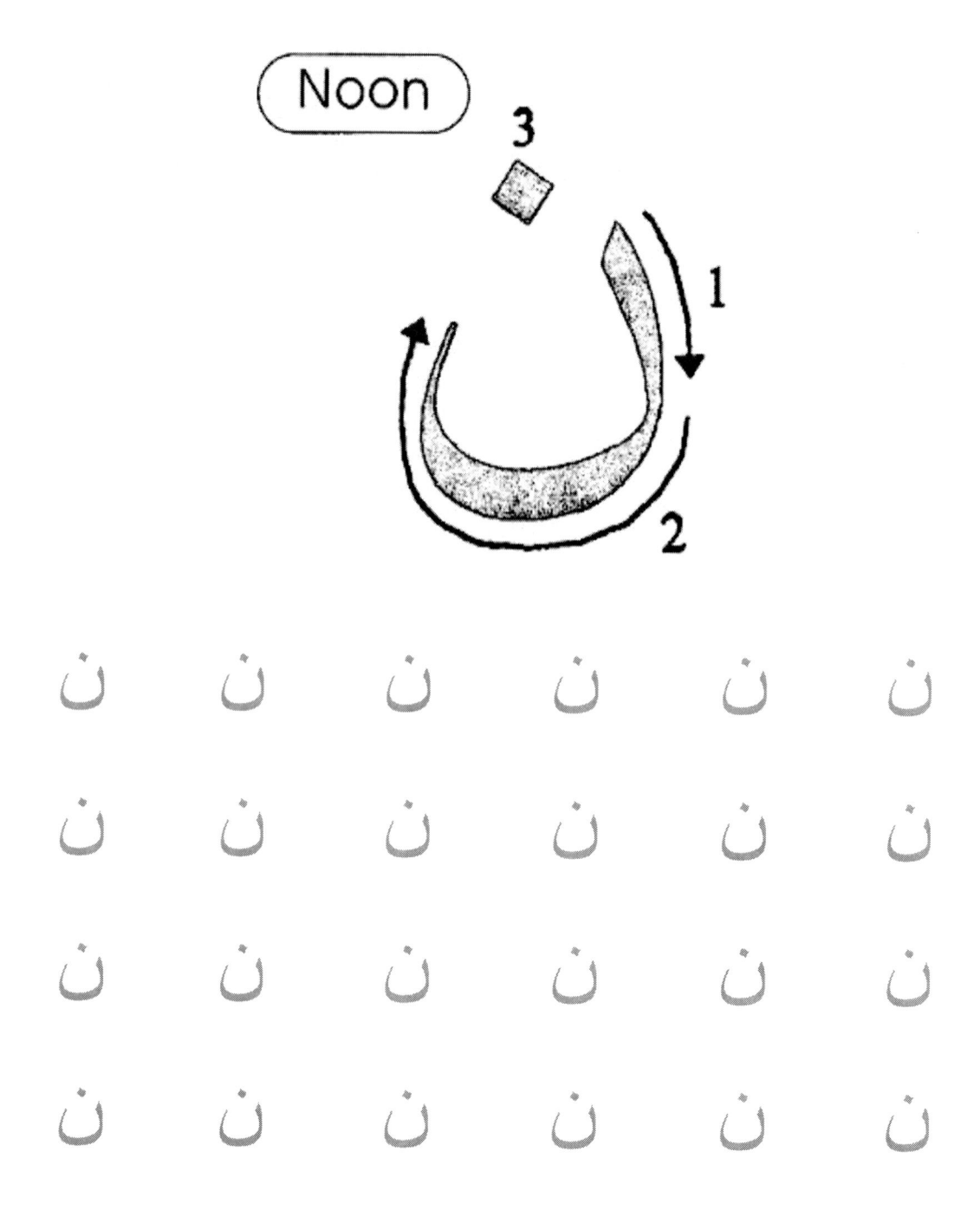

Noon

ن

Haa

Arabic Script

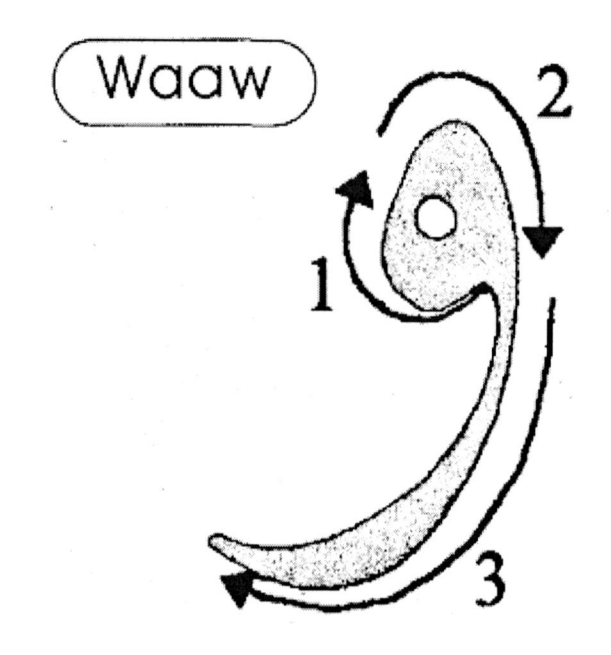

Waaw

و	و	و	و	و	و
و	و	و	و	و	و
و	و	و	و	و	و
و	و	و	و	و	و

Yaa

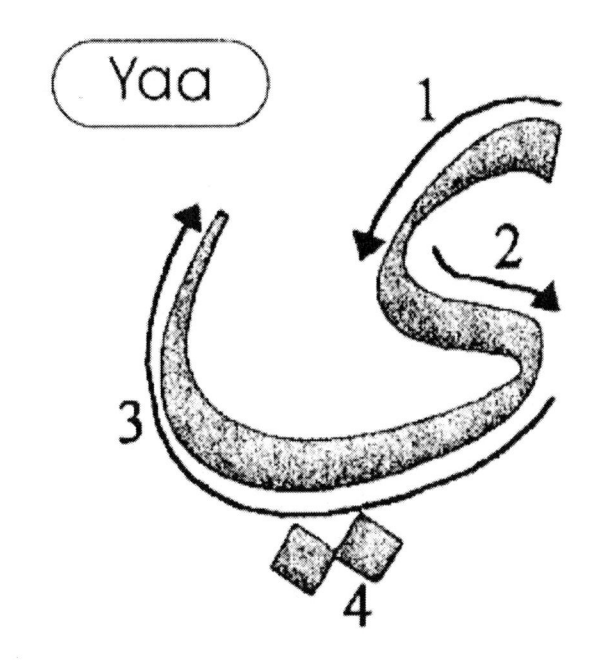

ي	ي	ي	ي	ي	ي
ي	ي	ي	ي	ي	ي
ي	ي	ي	ي	ي	ي
ي	ي	ي	ي	ي	ي

2-Yaa al-Madd is the long vowel lengthening the sound of the Kasra from 'i' into 'ee'. As in:

أي	بي	تي	ثي	جي	حي	خي
aee	bee	tee	thee	jee	Hee	Khee

3- Waaw al-Madd is the long vowel lengthening the sound of the Damma from 'u' into 'oo':

أو	بو	تو	ثو	جو	حو	خو
Aoo	boo	too	thoo	joo	Hoo	Khoo

sukun and shaddah

The **(Sukun)** is a shape of a circle and it's written above a letter to show that there is no vowel on the letter, as below:

Arabic Word	أَبْ	مِنْ	اِبْن
Translation	Father	From	Son
Transliteration	Ab	Min'	Ebn

The **(Shadda)** is a diacritical mark written above a letter to show that the letter has been doubled and therefore increases in emphasis as below:

Arabic Word	قِطَّة	بَطَّة	أُمّ
Translation	Cat	Duck	Mother
Transliteration	Qitta	Batta	Umm

- please note; the last letter of the words duck & cat is a different shape of the letter ta', you will see how it comes into this shape in the joining alphabet unit.

Arabic letters – Joined Form

Remember that Arabic is written from right to left, and Arabic alphabet can be joined like the cursive way of writing English, it just depends on the position of the letter in the word, if it is at the (beginning, middle or end). Dashes are added between letters to join them.

The easiest and quickest way to learn how to join Arabic letters is to put them into 6 groups, as shown below:

First group:

Unique letters - there are 6 letters which do not join to any other letter (but can be joined one side), so they are called one way connectors, these letters are:

أ   د   ذ   ر   ز   و

You will find them in different positions in the words, beginning, middle and end, as in next ;

By Itself	Not joined	End	Middle	Beginning	Letter
ا	ااا	ـا	ـا	ا	*Alif*
د	ددد	ـد	ـد	د	*daal*
ذ	ذذذ	ـذ	ـذ	ذ	*Thaal*
ر	ررر	ـر	ـر	ر	*Raa'*
ز	ززز	ـز	ـز	ز	*Zai*
و	ووو	ـو	ـو	و	*Waaw*

Second group:

ب ت ث ن ي

These are letters which have similar shapes **individually** (as you learnt earlier), this group is also similar in **joined** form (Baa, Taa',thaa' noon, and yaa'). The only difference in these letters is the number or positions of dots above or below the letter. Look at the next:

By Itself	Joined	End	Middle	Beginning	Letter
ب	بب	ـب	ـبـ	بـ	*Baa'*
ت	تت	ـت	ـتـ	تـ	*Taa'*
ث	ثث	ـث	ـثـ	ثـ	*Thaa'*
ن	نن	ـن	ـنـ	نـ	*Noon*
ي	يي	ـي	ـيـ	يـ	*Yaa'*

Third group:

ج ح خ ع غ

These letters also have the same rules of how to join them. Remember that any letters that have two parts (part written above the line & the other part is below the line) we cut the part which is below the line at a beginning of a word or in the middle. If that letter is located at the end it has to be written fully, as shown below:

By Itself	Joined	End	Middle	Beginning	Letter
ج	ججج	ـج	ـجـ	جـ	Jeem
ح	ححح	ـح	ـحـ	حـ	Haa'
خ	خخخ	ـخ	ـخـ	خـ	Khaa'
ع	ععع	ـع	ـعـ	عـ	'Ayn
غ	غغغ	ـغ	ـغـ	غـ	Ghayn

Fourth group:

ض ص ش س

If any letter has two parts (above and below the line) we don't need the part which is below, unless at the end of a word;

By Itself	Joined	End	Middle	Beginning	Letter
س	سسس	ـس	ـسـ	سـ	Seen
ش	ششش	ـش	ـشـ	شـ	Sheen
ص	صصص	ـص	ـصـ	صـ	Saad
ض	ضضض	ـض	ـضـ	ضـ	Daad

Fifth group:

ط ظ ف ق

This is the simplest one as nothing has to be changed. Dashes are just added to join them:

Letter	Beginning	Middle	End	Joined	By Itself
Taa'	ط	ـطـ	ـط	ططط	ط
Zaa'	ظ	ـظـ	ـظ	ظظظ	ظ
Faa'	ف	ـفـ	ـف	ففف	ف
Qaaf	ق	ـقـ	ـق	ققق	ق

The Sixth and last group:

ك ل م ه

There are very few changes in shape at beginning and in the middle of words

Letter:	Beginning:	Middle:	End:	Joined:	By Itself:
Kaaf	ک	ـک	ـک	ککک	ك
Laam	ل	ـلـ	ـل	لل	ل
Meem	مـ	ـمـ	ـم	مـمـم	م
Haa'	هـ	ـهـ	ـه	هەه	ه

50

There are two more shapes you can see in Arabic script. The first is a combination of the letters (lam & alif):

ل + ا

لا

Lam + alif

laa

The second shape is called (taa' marboota), and you can read it as (a). You will only find it at the end of 90 % of the Arabic feminine words as a mark to show that it's feminine:

ة like ذُرَة   ـة like بَطَّة

thura   batta

If you see yaa' at the end of a word, so read it as a long vowel (aa), but only at the end, as in the below two girls names:

لَيْلَى laylaa

لُبْنَى lubnaa

Reading Exercises

Exercise one: Practice reading the below words, of course from right to left, also the right side shows the letters individually.

Pay attention to letters that are joined after cutting the parts which are below the line, if the letter is at the beginning or in the middle of the words. You will find it written fully at the end in a cursive way as we learned earlier;

Meaning	Final Form	Changed Form	Letters individually
He read (past).	قَرَأ	قَـرَأ	ق رَ أ
He wrote.	كَتَبَ	كَـتَـبَ	كَ تَ بَ
He drank.	شَرِبَ	شَـرِبَ	شَ رِ بَ
He ate.	أكَلَ	أ كَـلَ	أ كَ لَ
He worked.	عَمَلَ	عَـمَـلَ	عَ مَ لَ
He understood.	فَهِمَ	فَـهِـمَ	فَ هِ مَ
He lived.	سَكَنَ	سَـكَـنَ	سَ كَ نَ
He went	ذَهَبَ	ذَ هَـبَ	ذَ هَ بَ
He attended	حَضَرَ	حَـضَـرَ	حَ ضَ رَ

Exercise two

practice reading

Simple words, just some of them has shaddah (doubled letter) as in mother, and (taa' marboota) as in grandmother;

Meaning	Final Form	Changed Form	Letters on their Own
Father.	أَبْ	أ بْ	أ بْ
Mother.	أَمّ	أ مّ	أ مّ
Brother.	أَخْ	أ خْ	أ خْ
Sister.	أَخْتْ	أ خْ تْ	أ خْ تْ
Son.	اِبْنْ	اِ بْ نْ	اِ بْ نْ
Daughter / girl.	بِنْتْ	بِ نْ تْ	بِ نْ تْ
Grandfather	جَدّ	جَ دّ	ج دّ
Grandmother	جَدَّة	جَ دَّ ة	جَ دَّ ة

Exercise three

Reading Exercises

Practice reading the below words. Pay attention to letters that are joined after cutting the parts which are below the line, if the letter is at the beginning or in the middle of the words. You will find it written fully at the end in a cursive way as we learned earlier;

Meaning	Final Form	Changed Form	Letters individually
He spent	قَضَى	قَـضَـى	ق ضَ ى
He walked	مَشَى	مَـشَـى	مَ شَ ى
He bought	اِشْتَرَى	اِشْـتَـرَى	اِشْ تَ رَ ى
He went	راحَ	راحَ	راحَ
He was	كانَ	كـانَ	ك ا نَ
He said	قالَ	قـالَ	ق ا لَ
He lived	عاشَ	عـاشَ	ع ا شَ
He died	ماتَ	مـاتَ	م ا تَ
He arrived	وَصَلَ	وَصَـلَ	وَ صَ لَ

Silent letters in Arabic

There is one other important rule to keep in mind when it comes to the definite article "*al*".

Remember the phrases "*as-salaam*" and "*an-nuur*" in first part of this book. As the "*as*" in "*as-salaam*" and the "*an*" in "*an-nuur*" means "the" as well, But as you can see how they pronounced differently from "*al*".

That's because there are few letters in Arabic when they come after the definite article "*al*" so they can cancel the pronunciation of the "*l*" sound in "*al*" and that time you will find only the "*a*" followed by those mentioned letters doubled, as in "*as-salaam*" with double "*s*" and "*an-nuur*" with double "*n*".

Those letters called "sun letters" because the word "*shams*" in Arabic which means "sun" begins with one of them.

How to know those letters? Simply they are the ones which we use the tip of the tongue to pronounce them: "*t , th , d , dh , r , z , sh , s, l, n*". Fourteen of the Arabic alphabets:

ت، ث، د، ذ، ر ، ز، س، ش، ص، ض، ط، ظ، ل، ن

The other 14 letters which don't force "*l*" in "*al*" to be silent are called "moon letters" because the word "moon" = in Arabic begins with one of them. Here is the example for both cases:

"*SabaaH*" = a morning, "*aS-SabaaH*" = the morning. "*Masaa'*" = an evening, "*al-masaa'*" = the evening. "*Shams*" = sun, "*ash-shams*" = the sun. "*qamar*" = moon, "*al-qamar*" = the moon. Next chart shows an example for each letter.

الحروف الشمسية Sun letters	Transliteration	Transliteration	الحروف القمرية Moon letters
التمر The dates	At-tamr	al-'abb	الأب The father
الثالث The third	ath-thaleth	al-baab	الباب The door
الدقيق The flour	ad-daqiiq	al-jamal	الجمل The camel
الذهب The gold	ATh-Thahb	al-Hadiiqa	الحديقة The park
الرجل The man	ar-rajul	al-khubz	الخبز The bread
الزهرة The flower	az-zahra	al-'Ayn	العين The eye
السمك The fish	as-samak	al-ghadaa'	الغداء The lunch
الشمس	ash-shams	al-famm	الفـم

The sun			The mouth
الصورة	aS-Suura	al-qamar	القمر
The picture			The moon
الضيف	aD-Dayf	al-ketaab	الكتاب
The guest			The book
الطالب	aT-Taaleb	al-mudar-res	المدرس
The student			The teacher
الظلام	aTH-THalaam	al-waqt	الوقت
The dark			The time
الليل	al-layl	al-hawaa'	الهواء
The night			The air
النور	An-nuur	al-yadd	اليد
The light			The hand

UNIT TWO

What is this?

Contents

- Demonstratives

- Useful adjectives

- Grammar and usage

- Simple sentences

- Noun-Adjective phrases

What's this?
maa haThaa / haThehe?

ما هَذا / هَذِهِ؟

Demonstratives

The demonstratives "*haTha / haThehe*" are translated as "this is a/an…." and "this…" and are used to refer to masculine and feminine nouns.

Look at the below examples and learn how to say "this is a" & "this is the":

1- **This is a / an**…. (referring to a masculine)

هَذا قَلَم
haTha qalam
This is a pen

هَذا كِتاب
haTha Ketaab
This is a book

هَذا بَيْت
haTha bayt
This is a house

هَذا هَاتِف
haTha haatef
This is a telephone

هَذا مَكْتَب
haTha maktab
This is an office / desk

هَذا كُرْسِي
haTha kursy
This is a chair

2- **This is a / an**....(referring to a feminine)

هَذِهِ سَيّارَة
haThehe say-yaara
This is a car

هَذِهِ غُرْفَة
haThehe ghurfa
This is a room

هَذِهِ بِنْت
haThehe bent
This is a girl

هَذِهِ صُورَة
haThehe Suura
This is a picture

هَذِهِ ساعَة
haThehe saaAa
This is a watch

هَذِهِ مَكْتَبة
haThehe maktaba
This is a library

1- **This**…. (referring to a masculine)

هَذا البَيْت	هَذا الكِتاب	هَذا القَلَم
haTha al-bayt	*haTha al-ketaab*	*haTha al-qalam*
This house	This book	This pen

هَذا الكُرْسي	هَذا المَكْتَب	هَذا الهَاتِف
haTha al-kursy	*haTha al-maktab*	*haTha al-haatef*
This chair	This office / desk	This telephone

2- **This**…. (referring to a feminine)

هَذِهِ البِنْت	هَذِهِ الغُرْفَة	هَذِهِ السَيّارَة
haThehe el-bent	*haThehe el-ghurfa*	*haThehe es-say-yaara*
This girl	This room	This car

هَذِهِ الطّاوِلَة	هَذِهِ السّاعَة	هَذِهِ الصُّورَة
haThehe eT-Taawela	*haThehe es-saaAa*	*haThehe eS-Suura*
This table	This watch	This picture

Useful adjectives:

Note that (m) is an abbreviation for (masculine) & (f) is abbreviation for (feminine). You can see that the basic rule in the Arabic language is to put "ة" "*taa marbuuta*" to the masculine adjective to make it feminine.

English	Transliteration	Arabic
b) big /(old for human)	*kabiir (m)*	كَبير
	kabiira (f)	كَبيرة
a) small	*Saghiir (m)*	صَغير
	Saghiira(f)	صَغيرة
a) far	*baAiid (m)*	بَعيد
	baAiida (f)	بَعيدة
b) near / close to	*qariib (m)*	قَريب
	qariiba (f)	قَريبة
b) old (not for human)	*qadiim (m)*	قَديم
	qadiima (f)	قَديمة
a) new	*jadiid (m)*	جَديد
	jadiida (f)	جَديدة

a) good	jay-yed (m)	جَيِّد
	jay-yeda (f)	جَيِّدة
b) bad	say-ye' (m)	سَيِّء
	say-ye'a (f)	سَيِّئة
a) wide	waaseA (m)	واسِعْ
	waaseAa (f)	واسِعَة
b) narrow	Day-yeq (m)	ضَيِّق
	Day-yeqa (f)	ضَيِّقَة
beautiful	jamiil (m)	جَميل
	jamiila (f)	جَميلة
nice	laTiif (m)	لَطيف
	laTiifa (f)	لَطيفة

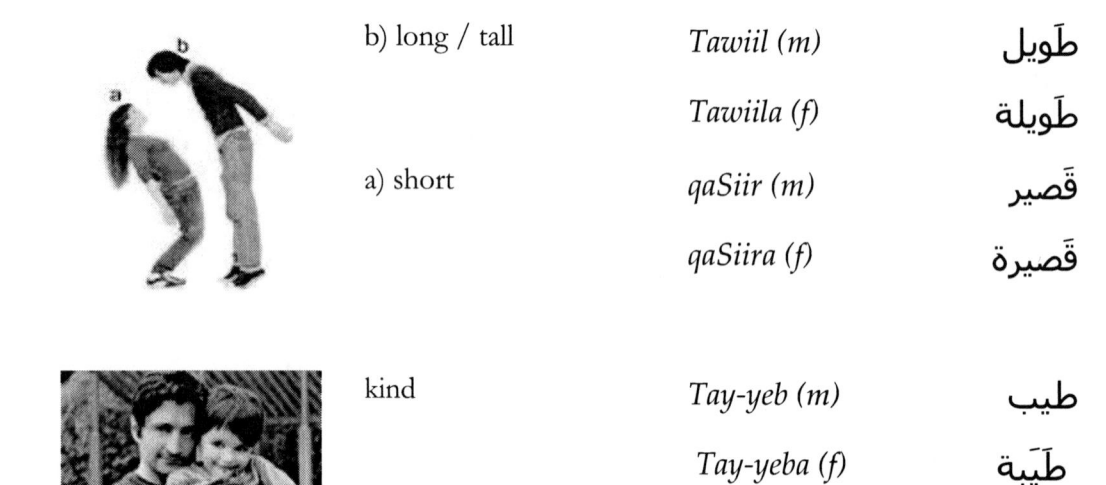

b) long / tall	Tawiil (m)	طَويل
	Tawiila (f)	طَويلة
a) short	qaSiir (m)	قَصير
	qaSiira (f)	قَصيرة
kind	Tay-yeb (m)	طَيب
	Tay-yeba (f)	طَيَبة

Grammar notice

Simple Sentences

Many Arabic sentences do not need the verb 'to be' (am, is, are) in the present tense, which means that you can have a 'nominal sentence' without verbs at all. Look at the following phrases;

أنا أَحْمَد	أنا مِنْ سوريا	أنا مُهَنْدِس
'anaa 'aHmad.	'anaa men suurya	'anaa muhandes
I (am) Ahmad.	I (am) from Syria	I (am) an engineer

هُوَ حَمْدان	هُوَ مِنْ قَطِر	هُوَ مُحاسِب
huwa Hamdaan	huwa men qatar	huwa muHaaseb
He (is) Hamdan	He (is) from Qatar	He (is) an accountant

نَحْنُ مِن الإمارات	أنْتُم مِن دُبَي	هُمْ مِن جَدّة
naHnu men al-emaaraat	'antum men dubai	hum men jad-da
We (are) from Emirates	You (are) all from Dubai	They (are) from Jeddah

البَيْت جَميل	الجَوّ لَطيف	المَدينَة كَبيرَة
al-bayt jamiil	al-jaww laTiif	al-madiina kabiira
The house (is) beautiful	The weather (is) nice	The city (is) big

Noun-Adjective phrases:

It is simple to form an adjective phrases in Arabic, because (**The adjective follows the noun**), as in the below example.

البَيْت الكَبير   بَيْت كَبير

al-bayt al-kabiir   *bayt kabiir*

the big house   a big house

As you see in the two examples, if the noun has a definite article (*al*) also the adjective must be with (*al*), and vice versa.

Remember that, if the first word or the noun is definite or with (*al*) and the second word is not definite, so; it will be considered a full nominal sentence as in the grammar notice number 1. Example;

البَيْت كَبير

al-bayt kabiir

The house (is) big

Personal pronouns:

Arabic is like English. It has two sets of personal pronouns: subject and possessive pronouns. There is some overlap among these sets. However, Arabic has more pronouns than English (Formal Arabic has separate categories for masculine and feminine and dual pronouns for sets of two, these are not used in most varieties of spoken Arabic). Here you will learn the following most commonly used subject pronouns in spoken Arabic:

I	'anaa	أنا
We	naHnu	نَحْنُ
You (for male)	'anta	أنْتَ
You (for female)	'anti	أنْتِ
You (plural)	'antum	أنتُم
He / It (for masculine)	huwa	هُوَ
She / It (for feminine)	heya	هِيَ
They (plural)	hum	هُم

Question words

To ask a question in Arabic, use one of the below words at the beginning of a sentence:

English	Transliteration	Arabic
What? (used before nouns)	maa	ما؟
What? (used before verbs)	maaThaa	ماذا؟
Why?	lema / lemaaThaa	لِمَ / لِماذا؟
Where?	'ayn	أينْ؟
Who?	man	مَنْ؟
When?	mataa	مَتى؟
How?	kayf	كَيْف؟
For (Yes/No) question	hal	هل؟
From where?	men 'ayn	مِنْ أين؟
With whom?	maAa man	مَعَ مَنْ؟
Which?	'ayy	أي؟

Examples:

English	Transliteration	Arabic
1- What's your name?	*maa esmuk?*	؟1- ما اِسْمُك
2- What do you do?	*matha taAmal?*	؟2- ماذا تَعْمَل
3- Why are you in Egypt?	*lema 'anta fii meSr?*	؟3- لِمَ أنتَ في مِصْر
4- Where's the University?	*'ayn al-jaameAa ?*	؟4- أيْن الجامِعَة
5- Who is Adam?	*man 'adam?*	؟5- مَنْ آدَم
6- When is the lesson?	*mataa ad-dars?*	.؟6- مَتى الدّرْس
7- How are things?	*kayf al-Haal?*	.؟7- كَيْف الحال
8- Are you from France?	*hal 'anta men Faransaa?*	؟8- هل أنْتَ مِنْ فَرَنْسا
9- Where are you from?		؟9- من أين أنت
10- Which country are you from?	*men 'ayn 'anta?* *men 'ayy balad 'anta?*	؟ 10- مِنْ أي بَلَد أنتَ

Possessive pronouns:

Possessive pronouns in Arabic are suffixes attached to the nouns:

my name : *esmii* اِسْمي   my brother: *akhii* أخي

your name: *esmka / esmke* اِسْمكَ / اِسْمكِ

Here are all these suffixes with their subject pronouns, applied on an example:

English	Transliteration	Arabic
my office	*maktabii*	مَكْتَبـي
our office	*maktabnaa*	مَكْتَبـنا
your office (for a male)	*maktabka / ak* (spoken)	مَكْتَبـكَ
your office (for a female)	*maktabke / ek* (spoken)	مَكْتَبـكِ
your office (for plural)	*maktabkum*	مَكْتَبـكُم
his office	*maktabhu*	مَكْتَبـهُ
her office	*maktabhaa*	مَكْتَبـها
their office	*maktabhum*	مَكْتَبـهُم

Notice that, the possessive pronouns (*ka*) and (*ke*) for your are pronounced as (*ak*) for male and (*ek*) for female in spoken Arabic.

Saying (to have) in Arabic

You have noticed Adam in the dialogue when he said (*Aendii muHaaDara*)= I have lecture. The pronoun forms which he used with the preposition are basically the same like the possessive pronouns forms which mentioned in the previous lesson. The following table introduces these endings with prepositions indicating the meaning of (to have) in Arabic.

SAYING TO HAVE: PREPOSITIONS WITH POSSESSIVE SUFFIXES

English	لِ	L	عِنْدَ	Aend	مَعَ	maAa
I have	لِي	lii	عِنْدِي	Aendii	مَعِي	maAii
We have	لَنا	lanaa	عِنْدَنا	Aendnaa	مَعَنا	maAanaa
You have (m)	لَكَ	laka	عِنْدَك	Aendka	مَعَك	maAaka
You have (f)	لَكِ	lake	عِنْدَك	Aendke	مَعَك	maAake
You have (pl)	لَكُم	lakum	عِنْدَكم	Aendkum	مَعَكم	maAakum
He has	لَهُ	lahu	عِنْدَهُ	Aendhu	مَعَهُ	maAahu
She has	لَها	lahaa	عِنْدَها	Aendhaa	مَعَها	maAahaa
They have	لَهُم	lahum	عِنْدَهم	Aendhum	مَعَهُم	maAahum

Three of these combinations form (to have) in Arabic. The difference in how they are used to express possession is:

- (***lii***) is used when referring to owning people: (lii 'akh) = I have a brother

- (***Aend***) is used when referring to owning objects: (Aendii say-yaara) = I have a car

- (***maAa***) is used for referring to owning something right now: (maAii dollar)= I have a dollar. While some Arabic speakers use (***Aend***) for all cases.

The below table shows the Arabic numbers from Zero to Ten

The numerals used in English are of Arabic origin, but Arabs nowadays use the Hindi ones sometimes, because of business ties with India in past.

Number	Transliteration	Arabic script	Arabic Numeral
0	Sefr	صِفْر	0
1	waHed	واحِد	1
2	'ethnaan/'ethnayn	اثنان / إِثْنَين	2
3	thalatha	ثَلاثَة	3
4	'arbaAa	أَرْبَعَة	4
5	khamsa	خَمْسة	5
6	set-ta	سِتّة	6
7	sabAa	سَبْعَة	7
8	thamaaneya	ثَمانِية	8
9	tesAa	تِسْعَة	9
10	Aashara	عَشَرَة	10

Days of the week are mostly driven from numbers as per the following table.

Days of the week

English	Transliteration	Arabic
Sunday	yawm mel-'aHad	يَوْم الأحَد
Monday	yawm el-ethnayn	يَوْم الإثْنَيْن
Tuesday	yawm ethulathaa'	يَوْم الثُّلاثاء
Wednesday	yawm el-arbeAa'	يَوْم الأرْبعاء
Thursday	yawm el-khamees	يَوْم الخَميس
Friday	yawm el-jumuAa	يَوْم الجُمعَة
Saturday	yawm as-sabt	يَوْم السَّبْت

Months

English	Transliteration	Arabic
January	*yanayer*	يناير
February	*fubrayer*	فبراير
March	*maares*	مارس
April	*'abriil*	ابريل
May	*mayuu*	مايو
June	*yuunyuu*	يونيو
July	*yuulyuu*	يوليو
August	*'aughusTus*	أغسطس
September	*sebtamber*	سبتمبر
October	*'auktober*	أكتوبر
November	*nuufamber*	نوفمبر
December	*diisamber*	ديسمبر

As you see the above table shows the Arabized months from the Latin ones. Also there are the Arabic months which used for the Islamic calendar. Thos months depend on the **lunar** calendar.

muHar-ram, Safar, rabiiA 'aw-wal, rabiiA thaanii, jumaad 'aw-wal, jumaad thaanii, rajab, shaAbaan, ramadaan, shaw-waal, Thu l-qeAda,

Thu l-Hej-ja.

مُحَرّم، صَفَر، رَبِيع أوّل، رَبِيع ثاني، جُماد أولى، جُمادى ثانية، رَجَب، شَعْبان، رَمَضان، شَوّال، ذو القِعْدة، ذو الحِجّة.

Arabic ordinal numbers can be easily distinguished from the numbers used in counting. The table below includes the numbers first to twelve; they are presented together with the definite article. This is the form used in telling the time.

Ordinal Numbers

English	Transliteration	Arabic
The first	al-'aw-wal	الأوّل
The second	ath-thaani	الثّاني
The third	ath-thaaleth	الثّالِث
The fourth	ar-raabeA	الرّايع
The fifth	al-khaames	الخامِس
The sixth	as-saades	السّادِس
The seventh	as-saabeA	السّايع
The eighth	ath-thaamen	الثّامِن
The ninth	at-taaseA	التّاسِع
The tenth	al-Aaasher	العاشِر
The eleventh	al-Hadii Aashar	الحادِي عَشَر
The twelfth	ath-thaanii Aashar	الثّاني عَشَر

Arabic - English glossary

The following glossary contains the words presented in this book. Also most of the meanings given are as used in the book. Plurals are given in brackets after singulars, and verbs are given in Arabic in present and past tenses.

English	Transliteration	Arabic
Son	*ebn*	اِبْن
Daughter	*ebna*	اِبْنَة
Nephew	*ebn akh*	اِبْن الأخ
Name	*esm*	اِسْم
my name	*esmy*	اِسْمي
woman	*emra'a*	اِمْرَأة
The (Definite article attached to the words).	*al*	اَلْ
condition	*al-Haal*	الْحَال
Night time	*al-layl*	اللَّيل
Daytime	*an-nahaar*	النَّهار
Light	*en-nuur*	النّور
Today	*al-yuum*	الْيَوْم
Exam	*al-emteHaan*	الامْتِحان
the Emirates	*al-'emaaraat*	الإمارات
blue	*al-'azraq*	الأَزْرق
white	*al'abyaD*	الأَبْيَض
black	*al'aswad*	الأَسْوَد

Dairy	al-'albaan	الألْبان
The father	al-'ab	الأب
now	al-'aan	الآن
Al-Basra	al-baSra	البَصْرَة
The door	al-baab	الباب
Shopping	at-tasaw-wuq	التَّسَوُّق
beauty	at-tajmiil	التّجْميل
The dates	at-tamr	التمر
the third	ath-thaaleth	الثالث
the weather	al-jaww	الجَوّ
Cheese	al-jubn	الجبن
The camel	al-jamal	الجمل
Praise	al-Hamd	الحَمْدُ
Thanks to <u>God</u>	al-Hamdulillah	الحَمْدُ لِله
the bus	alHaafela	الحافلة
The park	alHadiiqa	الحديقة
The bread	al-khubz	الخبز
The flour	ad-daqiiq	الدقيق
The gold	aTh-Thahab	الذهب
The man	ar-rajul	الرجل
The rose	az-zahra	الزهرة
Peace	as-salaam	السَّلامُ
Peace be upon you	as-salaam Aalaikum	السَّلام عَلَيْكُم
sweater	as-sutra	السّتْرة
Supermarket	as-suuper market	السُّوبر مارْكِت

77

The fish	as-samak	السمك
work	ash-shughl	الشُغْل
The sun	ash-shams	الشمس
Health	aS-she-Ha	الصّحَة
The picture	aS-Suura	الصورة
The guest	aD-Dayf	الضيف
The student	aT-Taaleb	الطالب
The dark	aTH-Thalaam	الظلام
the honey	al-Aasal	العسل
The eye	alAin	العين
launch	al-ghadaa'	الغَداء
the bill	al-faatuura	الفاتورَة
The mouth	al-fam	الفـم
Cairo	al-qaahera	القاهِرَة
menu	al-qaa'ema	القائمة
train	al-qeTaar	القطار
The moon	al-qamar	القمر
The book	al-ketaab	الكتاب
Allah (name of the God)	Allah	الله
God bless you	Allah yubaarek fiik	الله يُبارك فيك
the city	al-madiina	المَدينة
night	al-masaa'	المَساء
size	al-maqaas	المَقاسْ
The teacher	al-mudar-res	المدرس
waiter	an-naadel	النّادِل

success	an-najaaH	النَجَاح
The air	al-hawaa'	الهواء
The time	al-waqt	الوقت
The hand	al-yad	اليد
permission	eThn	إذْن
traffic lights	eshaaraat elmuruur	إشارات المرور
emirati	emaaraatyy	إماراتي
english	engliizyy	إنكليزي
I find	ajed	أجِد
red	aHmar	أحْمَر
green	akhDar	أخْضَر
supplies	adawaat	أدَوات
I pay	adfaA	أدْفَعْ
I drink	ashrab	أشْرب
yellow	aSfar	أصْفَر
sure	akiid	أكيد
american	amriikyy	أمْريكي
I / I'm	anaa	أنَا
You (for male)	anta	أنْتَ
You (for female)	anti	أنْتِ
I look	anThur	أنْظُر
welcome	ahlan wa sahlan	أهْلاً وَسَهْلاً
first	aw-walan	أوّلاً
also	ayDan	أيْضاً
where?	ayn	أيْن؟

Sister	ukht	أُخْت
rice	urz	أُرْز
I want	uriid	أريد
Mother	umm	أمٌّ
Father	ab	أبّ
Abu Dhabi	abuu Thaby	أبوظبي
Brother	akh	أخْ
family	usra	أسْرة
colors	alwaan	ألوان
German	almaanyy	ألمانيّ
Germany	almaanya	ألمانيا
America	amriika	أمريكا
You (plural)	antum	أنتُّم
Days	ay-yaam	أيّام
anything	'shaye ay-y	أيّ شَيء
Else	akhar	آخَر
I eat	aakul	آكُل
miss	aanesa	آنِسة
suit	badla	بَدلة
after	baAd	بَعْد
far	baAiid/a	بَعيد / بَعيدة
pants	banTaluun	بَنْطَلون
Home	bayt	بَيْت
orange	burtuqaal	بُرْتَقال
Orange	burtuqaalyy	بُرْتَقالي
Brown	bun-nyy	بنّي

80

Good	*bekhayr*	يَخْير
without	*beduun*	يَدُون
girl	*bent*	يْنت
cold	*baared*	بارد
certainly	*bet-ta'akiid*	بالتَّأكيد
seller	*baa'eA*	بائع
blouse	*buluuza*	بلوزة
translation	*tarjama*	تَرْجمَة
Honored to meet you	*tashar-rafna*	تَشَرَّفْنا
Please	*tafaD-Dal*	تَفَضَّل
Wake up in good condition	*tusbeH Aalaa khayr*	تُصْيح عَلى خَيْر
telephone	*telefuun*	تليفون
ice	*thalj*	تَلْج
University	*jaameAa*	جَامِعَة
Grandfather	*jadd*	جَدّ
Grandmother	*jad-da*	جَدَّة
new	*jadiid/a*	جَديد / جَديدة
beautiful	*jamiil/a*	جَميل / جَميلة
hungry	*jawAaan*	جَوْعان
socks	*jawaareb*	جوارب
good	*jay-yed/a*	جَيّد / جَيّدة
hot	*Haar*	حَارّ
shoe	*HeThaa'*	حِذاء
story	*Hekaaya*	حِكايَة
Computer	*Haasuub*	حاسوب

81

English	Transliteration	Arabic
milk	Haliib	حليب
sale	KhaSm	خَصْم
uncle / aunt	khaal/a	خال/ة
chicken	dajaaj	دَجَاج
Dubai	dubai	دُبَي
Dirhm	derham	درهم
Dollar	duulaar	دولار
Golden	Thahabyy	ذَهَبي
message	resaala	رسَالة
tie	rabTat Aunuq	ربطة عُنّق
sad	zaAlaan	زَعْلان
Pink	zahryy	زَهْري
bottle	zujaaja	زجَاجة
happy	saAiid/a	سَعِيد/ سَعِيدة
salad	salaTa	سَلَطة
your safety	salaamatk	سَلامتك
bad	say-ye'/a	سَيِّء / سَيِّئة
car	say-yaara	سَيّارَة
sugar	suk-kar	سُكّر
Syria	suurya	سُوريا
market/ super market	suuq	سُوق
hot	saakhen	سَاخِن
watch	saaAa	ساعَة
thank you	shukran	شُكْرًا
Morning	SabaaH	صَباح
friend	Sadiiq	صَديق

82

English	Transliteration	Arabic
small / young	Saghiir/a	صَغير / صَغيرة
page	SafHa	صَفْحَة
picture	Suura	صُورَة
tight	Day-yeq	ضَيْق
table	Taawela	طَاوِلَة
of course	TabAan	طَبْعًا
Scarf	TarHa	طَرحة
tall	Tawiil/a	طَويل / طَويلة
child	Tefl	طِفْل
student	Taaleb	طَالِب
kind	Tay-yeb/a	طَيِب / طَيَبة
juice	AaSiir	عَصير
Excuse me	Aafwan	عَفوًا
Iraqi	Aeraaqyy	عِراقيّ/ة
at	Aenda	عِنْدَ
habbit	Aaada	عادَة
flag	Aalam	علم
the dressing room	ghurfat l-qeyaas	غُرْفَة القياس
Room	ghurfa	غرفَة
France	faransaa	فَرَنْسا
french	faransyy	فَرَنْسي
Class	faSl	فَصْل
Nice to meet you	furSa saAiida	فُرْصة سعيدة
dress	fustaan	فُستان
Silver (color)	feD-Dyy	فِضّي

83

really	feAlan	فِعْلا
in	fii	في
old	qadiim/a	قَديم / قَديمة
near	qariib/a	قَريب / قَريبة
short	qaSiir/a	قَصير / قَصيرة
Quatar	qaTar	قَطَر
Qatari	qaTaryy	قَطَري/ة
Pen	qalam	قَلَم
little	qaliilan	قَليلا
Shirt	qamiiS	قَميص
department / section	qesm	قِسْم
coffee	qahwa	قهوة
big	kabiir	كَبير
canada	kanada	كَنَدا
how	kayf	كَيْف
Chair	kursyy	كُرسِي
everything	kul shaye'	كُلْ شَيْء
college/ faculty	kul-ley-ya	كُلية
Kuwaiti	kuwiityy	كُويتي
enough	kaaf	كاف
meat	laHm	لَحْم
Nice	laTiif/a	لَطيف / لَطيفة
but	laaken	لَكِن
Good night	layla saAiida	لَيْلة سَعيدة
One night	layla	لَيْلة
lebanon	lubnaan	لُبْنان

for	le	لِ
why?	lema / lemaThaa	لِمَ / لِماذا؟
no	laa	لا
actor	mumath-thel	مُمثِّل
congratulation	mabruuk	مَبْروك
when?	mataa	مَتى؟
School	madrasa	مَدْرسة
welcome	marHaba	مَرْحَبًا
Woman	mar'a	مَرأة
Evening	masaa'	مَساء
busy	mashghuul	مَشْغول
famous	mash-huur	مَشْهور
restaurant	maTAam	مَطْعَم
with	maAa	مَعَ
good bye	maAas-salaama	مَعَ السَّلامَة.
with whom?	maAa man?	مَعَ مَنْ؟
office/ desk	maktab	مَكْتَب
corridor / aisle	mamarr	مَمَرّ
who?	man	مَنْ؟
clever	mujtahed	مُجْتَهِد
lecture	muHaaDara	مُحاضَرة
accountant	muHaaseb	مُحاسِب
different	mukhtalefa	مُخْتَلِفة
director/manager	mudiir	مُدير
exhausted	murhaq	مُرهَق

muslim	muslem	مُسْلِم
possible	mumken	مُمْكِن
engeneer	muhandes	مُهَنْدِس
Clerk	muwaTH-THaf	مُوَظَّف
Egypt	meSr	مِصْر
Egyptian	meSryy	مِصْرِي
Seat	meqAad	مَقْعَد
salt	melH	مِلْح
From	men	مِنْ
from where?	men 'ayn?	مِنْ أَيْن؟
Please	men faDlek	مِنْ فَضْلِك
what? (used before nouns)	maa?	ما؟
water	meyaah / 'maa	ماء / مِياه
what? (used before verbs)	maaThaa	ماذا؟
station	maHaT-Ta	محطة
We	naHnu	نَحْنْ
a look	naTHra	نَظْرَة
yes	naAam	نَعَمْ
same	nafs	نَفْس
number	nemra	نِمْرَة
telephone	haatef	هَاتِف
this(f)	haaThehe	هَذِهِ
this (m)	haaThaa	هَذا
a word for yes / no question	hal	هَلْ
They (plural)	hum	هَم
He / It (for masculine)	huwa	هُوَ

She /It (for feminine)	heya	هِيَ
and	wa	و
paper	waraqa	وَرَقَة
wide	waaseA/a	واسِعْ / واسِعَة
take	ya'khuTh	يَأخُذ
eat	ya'kul	يَأكُل
it seems	yabduu	يَبدو
to Sit	yajles	يَجلِس
to Exit-go out	yakhruj	يَخرُج
to study	yadrus	يَدرُس
to live	yaskun	يَسكُن
to drink	yashrab	يَشرَب
to order	yaTlub	يَطلُب
to Know	yaAref	يَعرف
to Work	yaAmal	يَعمل
to understand	yafham	يَفهم
to sleep	yanaam	يَنَام
Day	yawm	يَومٌ
to try	yujar-reb	يُجَرِّب
to like	yuHeb	يُحِبّ
want	yuriid	يُريد
to through	yulqii	يُلقي

possible to	yumken 'an	يُمْكِن أن
vocative partcile	yaa	يا
to speak	yatakal-lam	يتكلم
to travel	yusaafer	يسافر

English - Arabic glossary

The following glossary contains the words presented in this book. Also most of the meanings given are as used in the book. Plurals are given in brackets after singulars, and verbs are given in Arabic in present and past tenses.

English	Transliteration	Arabic
a look	naTHra	نَظْرَة
a word for yes / no question	hal	هَلْ
Abu Dhabi	abuu Thaby	أبوظبي
accountant	muHaaseb	مُحاسِب
actor	mumath-thel	مُمثِل
after	baAd	بَعْد
Al-Basra	al-baSra	البَصْرَة
Allah (name of the God)	Allah	الله
also	ayDan	أَيْضًا
America	amriika	أمريكا
american	amriikyy	أمْريكي
and	wa	و

anything	shaye ay-y	أيّ شَيء
at	Aenda	عِنْدَ
bad	say-ye'/a	سَيّء / سَيّئة
beautiful	jamiil/a	جَميل / جَميلة
beauty	at-tajmiil	التَّجْميل
big	kabiir	كَبير
black	al'aswad	الأسْوَد
blouse	buluuza	بلوزة
blue	al-'azraq	الأَزْرَق
bottle	zujaaja	زُجاجة
Brother	akh	أخْ
Brown	bun-nyy	بُنّي
busy	mashghuul	مَشْغول
but	laaken	لَكِن
Cairo	al-qaahera	القاهِرَة
canada	kanada	كَنَدا
car	say-yaara	سَيّارَة
certainly	bet-ta'akiid	بالتَّأكيد
Chair	kursyy	كُرسي
Cheese	al-jubn	الجُبْن
chicken	dajaaj	دَجَاج
child	Tefl	طِفْل
Class	faSl	فَصْل
Clerk	muwaTH-THaf	مُوَظَّف
clever	mujtahed	مُجْتَهِد

coffee	qahwa	قهوة
cold	baared	بارد
college/ faculty	kul-ley-ya	كُلية
colors	alwaan	ألْوان
Computer	Haasuub	حاسوب
condition	al-Haal	الْحَال
congratulation	mabruuk	مَبْروك
corridor / aisle	mamarr	ممر
Dairy	al-'albaan	الألْبان
Daughter	ebna	إِبْنَة
Day	yawm	يَوْم
Days	ay-yaam	أيّام
Daytime	an-nahaar	النَّهار
department / section	qesm	قِسْم
different	mukhtalefa	مُخْتَلِفة
director/manager	mudiir	مُدير
Dirhm	derham	درهم
Dollar	duulaar	دولار
dress	fustaan	فُستان
Dubai	dubai	دُبَي
eat	ya'kul	يَأكُل
Egypt	meSr	مِصر
Egyptian	meSryy	مِصري
Else	akhar	آخَر
emirati	emaaraatyy	إماراتي
engeneer	muhandes	مُهَنْدِس

90

english	engliizyy	إنكليزي
enough	kaaf	كاف
Evening	masaa'	مَساء
everything	kul shaye'	كُلْ شَيْء
Exam	al-emteHaan	الامْتِحان
Excuse me	Aafwan	عَفوًا
exhausted	murhaq	مُرْهَق
family	usra	أسْرة
famous	mash-huur	مَشْهور
far	baAiid/a	بَعيد / بَعيدة
Father	ab	أبّ
first	aw-walan	أوْلاً
flag	Aalam	علم
for	le	لِ
France	faransaa	فَرَنْسا
french	faransyy	فَرَنْسي
friend	Sadiiq	صَديق
From	men	مِنْ
from where?	men 'ayn?	مِنْ أين؟
German	almaanyy	ألمانيّ
Germany	almaanya	ألمانيا
girl	bent	بِنْت
God bless you	Allah yubaarek fiik	الله يُبارك فيك
Golden	Thahabyy	ذَهَبي
Good	bekhayr	يِخَيْر

good	jay-yed/a	جَيِّد / جَيِّدة
good bye	maAas-salaama	مَعَ السَّلامَة.
Good night	layla saAiida	لَيْلَة سَعيدة
Grandfather	jadd	جَدّ
Grandmother	jad-da	جَدَّة
green	akhDar	أخْضَر
habbit	Aaada	عادَة
happy	saAiid/a	سَعيد/ سَعيدة
He / It (for masculine)	huwa	هُوَ
Health	aS-she-Ha	الصِّحَة
Home	bayt	بَيْت
Honored to meet you	tashar-rafna	تَشَرَّفْنا
hot	Haar	حَارّ
hot	saakhen	ساخِن
how	kayf	كَيْف
hungry	jawAaan	جَوْعان
I / I'm	anaa	أنَا
I drink	ashrab	أشْرَب
I eat	aakul	آكُل
I look	anThur	أنْظُر
I pay	adfaA	أدْفَعْ
I want	uriid	أريد
ice	thalj	ثَلْج
in	fii	في
Iraqi	Aeraaqyy	عِراقيّ/ة
it seems	yabduu	يَبْدو

English	Transliteration	Arabic
juice	AaSiir	عَصير
kind	Tay-yeb/a	طيب / طَيِّبة
Kuwaiti	kuwiityy	كُويتي
launch	al-ghadaa'	الغَداء
lebanon	lubnaan	لُبْنان
lecture	muHaaDara	مُحَاضَرَة
Light	en-nuur	النّور
little	qaliilan	قَليلا
market/ super market	suuq	سُوق
meat	laHm	لَحْم
menu	al-qaa'ema	القائمة
message	resaala	رسَالة
milk	Haliib	حليب
miss	aanesa	آنسة
Morning	SabaaH	صَباحْ
Mother	umm	أُمّ
muslim	muslem	مُسْلِم
my name	esmy	إِسْمي
Name	esm	إِسْم
near	qariib/a	قَريب / قَريبة
Nephew	ebn akh	إِبْن الأخ
new	jadiid/a	جَديد / جَديدة
Nice	laTiif/a	لطيف / لطيفة
Nice to meet you	furSa saAiida	فُرْصة سعيدة
night	al-masaa'	المَساء

93

Night time	al-layl	الْلَيل
no	laa	لا
now	al-'aan	الآن
number	nemra	نِمْرَة
of course	TabAan	طَبعًا
office/ desk	maktab	مَكْتَب
old	qadiim/a	قَديم / قَديمة
One night	layla	لَيْلة
orange	burtuqaal	بُرْتقال
Orange	burtuqaalyy	بُرْتقالي
page	SafHa	صَفْحَة
pants	banTaluun	بَنْطَلون
paper	waraqa	وَرَقَة
Peace	as-salaam	السَّلامُ
Peace be upon you	as-salaam Aalaikum	السَّلام عَلَيْكُم
Pen	qalam	قَلَم
permission	eThn	إذْن
picture	Suura	صُورَة
Pink	zahryy	زَهْري
Please	tafaD-Dal	تَفَضَّل
Please	men faDlek	مِنْ فَضْلِك
possible	mumken	مُمْكِن
possible to	yumken 'an	يُمْكِن أن
Praise	al-Hamd	الحَمْدُ
Qatari	qaTaryy	قَطَريّ/ة

Quatar	qaTar	قَطَر
really	feAlan	فِعْلا
red	aHmar	أحْمَر
restaurant	maTAam	مَطْعَم
rice	urz	أرز
Room	ghurfa	غرْفة
sad	zaAlaan	زَعْلان
salad	salaTa	سَلْطة
sale	KhaSm	خَصْم
salt	melH	مِلْح
same	nafs	نَفْس
Scarf	TarHa	طَرحة
School	madrasa	مَدْرسة
Seat	meqAad	مِقْعَد
seller	baa'eA	بائع
She /It (for feminine)	heya	هِي
Shirt	qamiiS	قَميص
shoe	HeThaa'	حِذاء
Shopping	at-tasaw-wuq	التَّسَوُّق
short	qaSiir/a	قَصير / قَصيرة
Silver (color)	feD-Dyy	فِضّي
Sister	ukht	أخْت
size	al-maqaas	المَقاس
small / young	Saghiir/a	صَغير / صَغيرة
socks	jawaareb	جَوارب

Son	ebn	إِبْن
station	maHaT-Ta	محطة
story	Hekaaya	حِكَايَة
student	Taaleb	طَالِب
success	an-najaaH	النَجَاح
sugar	suk-kar	سُكَّر
suit	badla	بَدْلة
Supermarket	as-suuper market	السُّوبر مارْكِت
supplies	adawaat	أَدَوات
sure	akiid	أكيد
sweater	as-sutra	السُّتْرَة
Syria	suurya	سُوريا
table	Taawela	طَاوِلَة
take	ya'khuTh	يَأخُذ
tall	Tawiil/a	طَويل / طَويلة
telephone	telefuun	تليفون
telephone	haatef	هَاتِف
thank you	shukran	شُكْرًا
Thanks to God	al-Hamdulillah	الحَمْدُ لله
The (Definite article attached to the words).	al	الْ
The air	al-hawaa'	الهواء
the bill	al-faatuura	الفَاتورَة
The book	al-ketaab	الكتاب
The bread	al-khubz	الخبز
the bus	alHaafela	الحافلة

The camel	al-jamal	الجمل
the city	al-madiina	المَدينَة
The dark	aTH-Thalaam	الظلام
The dates	at-tamr	التمر
The door	al-baab	الباب
the dressing room	ghurfat l-qeyaas	غُرْفَة القِياس
the Emirates	al-'emaaraat	الإمارات
The eye	alAin	العين
The father	al-'ab	الأب
The fish	as-samak	السمك
The flour	ad-daqiiq	الدقيق
The gold	aTh-Thahab	الذهب
The guest	aD-Dayf	الضيف
The hand	al-yad	اليد
the honey	al-Aasal	العسل
The man	ar-rajul	الرجل
The moon	al-qamar	القمر
The mouth	al-fam	الفم
The park	alHadiiqa	الحديقة
The picture	aS-Suura	الصورة
The rose	az-zahra	الزهرة
The student	aT-Taaleb	الطالب
The sun	ash-shams	الشمس
The teacher	al-mudar-res	المدرس
the third	ath-thaaleth	الثالث

The time	al-waqt	الوقت
the weather	al-jaww	الجوّ
They (plural)	hum	هُم
this (m)	haaThaa	هَذا
this (f)	haaThehe	هَذِهِ
tie	rabTat Aunuq	ربطة عُنُق
tight	Day-yeq	ضَيْق
to drink	yashrab	يَشْرَب
to Exit-go out	yakhruj	يَخْرُج
to Know	yaAref	يَعْرف
to like	yuHeb	يُحِبّ
to live	yaskun	يَسْكُن
to order	yaTlub	يَطْلُب
to Sit	yajles	يَجْلِس
to sleep	yanaam	يَنام
to speak	yatakal-lam	يتكلم
to study	yadrus	يَدْرُس
to through	yulqii	يُلْقي
to travel	yusaafer	يسافر
to try	yujar-reb	يُجَرّب
to understand	yafham	يَفْهم
to Work	yaAmal	يَعْمل
Today	al-yuum	الْيَوْم
traffic lights	eshaaraat elmuruur	إشارات المرور
train	al-qeTaar	القطار
translation	tarjama	تَرْجَمَة

uncle / aunt	khaal/a	خال/ة
University	jaameAa	جَامِعَة
vocative partcile	yaa	يا
waiter	an-naadel	النَادِل
Wake up in good condition	tusbeH Aalaa khayr	تُصْبِح عَلَى خَيْر
want	yuriid	يُرِيد
watch	saaAa	ساعَة
water	meyaah /'maa	ماء / مِياه
We	naHnu	نَحْنُ
welcome	ahlan wa sahlan	أَهْلاً وَسَهْلاً
welcome	marHaba	مَرْحَبًا
what? (used before nouns)	maa?	ما؟
what? (used before verbs)	maaThaa	ماذا؟
when?	mataa	مَتى؟
where?	ayn	أَيْن؟
white	al'abyaD	الأَبْيَض
who?	man	مَنْ؟
why?	lema / lemaThaa	لِمَ / لِماذا؟
wide	waaseA/a	واسِعْ / واسِعَة
with	maAa	مَعَ
with whom?	maAa man?	مَعَ مَنْ؟
without	beduun	يدُون
woman	emra'a	إمرَأة
Woman	mar'a	مَرْأة
work	ash-shughl	الشُغْل

yellow	*aSfar*	أَصْفَر
yes	*naAam*	نَعَمْ
You (plural)	*antum*	أنتُم
You (for female)	*anti*	أنْتِ
You (for male)	*anta*	أنْتَ
your safety	*salaamatk*	سَلامتك

ABOUT THE AUTHOR

The author has the pen name of Dr. Adam Yacoub, He is an experienced Arabic linguist, graduated from Al-Azhar University in Cairo, which is considered the third oldest Islamic university in the world (one thousand years-old foundation). He has worked also for several years in teaching Arabic as a foreign language, editor, and proofreader.

Arabic Script

CPSIA information can be obtained at www.ICGtesting.com
Printed in the USA
BVOW031630220512

290838BV00007B/22/P

9 781467 981460